CONTEMPORARY'S

W9-AQF-527

1/20
Edu

How to Teach Reading

For Teachers and Tutors

How to Teach Reading

For Teachers and Tutors

Edward Fry, Ph.D.

CONTEMPORARY BOOKS

a division of NTC/CONTEMPORARY PUBLISHING GROUP
Lincolnwood, Illinois USA

ISBN: 0-8092-9753-1

Published by Contemporary Books,
a division of NTC/Contemporary Publishing Group, Inc.,
4255 West Touhy Avenue,
Lincolnwood (Chicago), Illinois 60712-1975, U.S.A.
© 2000 by Edward Fry
All rights reserved. No part of this publication may be reproduced,
stored in a retrieval system, or transmitted in any form or by any means,
electronic, mechanical, photocopying, recording, or otherwise,
without prior permission of the publisher.
Manufactured in the United States of America.
3 4 5 6 7 8 9 0 VLP VLP 0 5 4 3 2 1

CONTENTS

PREFACE

The first draft of this book was developed at the Graduate School of Education at Rutgers University for a group of Peace Corps volunteers in training on campus. Their schedules were so crowded that little time was allotted for lectures on how to teach reading, so I thought it best to give them something to carry into the field when needed.

I later discovered that there were many people who wanted to know how to teach reading but who didn't want to take a full university course, or even read a thick teacher's textbook. So I rewrote the first draft into this basic manual.

This book has been used by thousands of adult literacy tutors, volunteers in programs for the disadvantaged, teachers' aides, parents, and even classroom teachers who want a rapid overview of some proven methods of teaching reading. It has also been used by college students in the reading laboratory and clinic portions of their teacher training courses.

The current revision reflects some changes in the reading field, including added emphasis on the use of quality literature for reading content and increased emphasis on writing. This new manual also has expanded lists of phonics words, high-frequency words, and lists of reading materials. Most important, however, the manual's six basic steps in teaching reading have stood the test of time, and I am pleased to know that they have helped thousands of students greatly improve their basic reading skills.

Edward Fry, Ph.D.
Professor Emeritus
Rutgers University

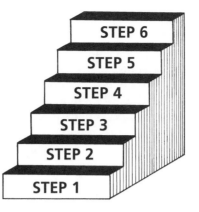

STEP 6
STEP 5
STEP 4
STEP 3
STEP 2
STEP 1

OVERVIEW

How to Teach Reading

How do you teach someone to read?

This is both an easy question and a difficult one. It can be answered in a sentence, in a paragraph, in a chapter, and in an entire book. Yet there would still be much more to say.

But just to make good on the opening statement, here is a one-sentence description of how you teach a student to read.

"You teach a student to read by helping him or her to learn the relationship between the printed words and their meanings."

If you say that is not much of an explanation, you are right. But even this brief explanation states a very basic concept underlying most reading instruction.

How about a one-paragraph answer to the opening statement:

"The teaching of reading usually begins by presenting the student with a story or passage that has simple vocabulary arranged in short, easy sentences. The student is given help and is encouraged to practice the sentences aloud and silently. More words are added to the reading material, and the sentences and passages get longer. Phonics skills, or the relationship between letters and sounds, are taught. Comprehension skills are taught usually by having the student read silently and answer various types of questions. Writing is introduced; the student starts to write and read his or her own stories or short passages. The printed passages, student-written material, phonics lessons, and comprehension activities gradually increase in difficulty as the student gains skill and fluency. Usually, a good deal of reading practice and frequent review lessons are necessary."

Although you probably found the one-paragraph explanation of teaching reading more satisfactory than that of one-sentence, it still does not give you too much insight into the reading process or specific methods of teaching reading. What follows is a one-chapter explanation in six steps, each of which is expanded to its own chapter. Most chapters include teaching resources. The book concludes with an Appendix of additional information that most teachers and tutors should find helpful.

This book is written from the standpoint of a teacher or tutor working with an individual student. Certainly, many of the methods discussed here apply to small groups and adult basic education (ABE) classes in reading, but to understand the reading process, it is important to consider what happens to "a student," not to some vague entity called "a group."

How to Teach Reading presents methods that are suitable for beginners and students with underdeveloped reading skills of young adult age through adulthood. The reading skills needed are the same for any beginning reader—practice with simple reading material, learning common words, basic phonics, and comprehension. The main difference in the process between children, teenagers, and adults is in the content of the reading material. For example, children might like fairy tales, whereas older and adult readers might prefer to read the newspaper or best-selling novels. Above all, developing readers need to know that learning to read and write is more than just moving through grade levels and worksheets. It is learning to create and understand meaning.

■ Step 1. Determine the Student's Reading Ability

The first thing to determine is the current reading level of the student. Do not go by the learner's age or years of schooling, factors that have only a general correlation with reading skills. Find out for yourself as closely as possible what level of material the student can read successfully. This can be done quickly and easily by using the **Oral Reading Test** (Appendix, page 106) and other informal methods, discussed in the full chapter on Step 1.

Oral Reading Test—Examples

Easy 1st Grade Difficulty Level:
Look at the dog.
It is big.
It can run.
Run, dog, run away.

5th Grade Difficulty Level:
High in the hills they came to a wide ledge where trees grew among the rocks. Grass grew in patches and the ground was covered with bits of wood from trees blown over a long time ago and dried by the sun. Down in the valley it was already beginning to get dark.

■ Step 2. Select the Right Reading Material

After you have determined your student's reading level, select or create reading material at the appropriate level. You can determine the grade equivalency level for any selection you think he or she should read by simply using the Readability Graph on page 13. In other words, this step shows you how to match the reading ability of the student with the difficulty level of the material. You should really do a careful and accurate job of matching at this point because the farther off you are from the correct match, the more difficult your teaching job will be; the closer the match, the easier it will be.

Another useful but less formal way of determining whether the reading material is at the proper level for the student is simply to ask him to read some of it aloud. The guidelines below will help you quickly judge the difficulty level of the material by the number of errors the student makes while reading it orally.

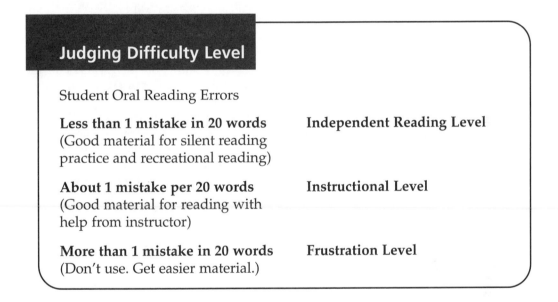

Judging Difficulty Level

Student Oral Reading Errors

Less than 1 mistake in 20 words   **Independent Reading Level**
(Good material for silent reading
practice and recreational reading)

About 1 mistake per 20 words   **Instructional Level**
(Good material for reading with
help from instructor)

More than 1 mistake in 20 words   **Frustration Level**
(Don't use. Get easier material.)

It is important that you know *why* your students are in a reading program and what they want to read. Whether it's to help their children with homework, read work-related materials, take a driving test, or enjoy romance or mystery novels, doing an inventory of students' interests, immediate reading needs, and longer-term goals will help you select relevant material for lessons, reading for life skills, and reading for pleasure.

■ Step 3. Have the Student Read Aloud and Silently for Comprehension

Once you have found the student's reading level and matched it with the correct reading material, what do you do? You have him read the material aloud, helping him as often as necessary. You also must have him practice reading silently, helping him if he needs it. This can be accomplished one on one or in a group setting.

Keep these practice lessons short so that the student does not become bored or frustrated. Schedule them regularly and frequently. To maintain your student's interest, vary the presentation of the material. You can present it on charts, on cards, in the context of games, on a sheet of paper, or by using a story or passage in a book.

There is no point in having students read—aloud or silently—if they don't understand what they are reading; the whole purpose of reading is to absorb the author's ideas. With beginning readers, teaching comprehension is usually not too difficult. These readers' speaking and listening vocabularies are so far beyond their reading vocabulary that comprehension takes place almost automatically when you show them the relationship between written and spoken language.

As reading skills develop over time, however, comprehension becomes a major concern and is usually taught specifically. Oral or written questions following oral or silent reading is the usual method.

Students simply cannot learn to read with comprehension unless they practice. Give them enough time to practice reading orally and silently for comprehension. Do not, however, make this an excuse for giving a lot of boring drills.

You can use variety to keep reading lessons moving. Go from oral reading to silent reading comprehension questions and exercises and then to the methods for teaching basic sight vocabulary (Instant Words, in Step 4) and phonics. Teachers and tutors should plan three or four different reading activities per hour or class session.

Of course, one of the best methods of practice is simply to find a book that engages the student and let him or her read it. Usually, getting a student to read silently for a long period of time requires finding a book that is a bit on the easy side. For this kind of pleasure reading, help the student select a book that is easier than one you would use for instruction. Your encouragement, visits to the library, assignment of oral or written discussion questions or summaries of the reading, and so on, will motivate your student to read on his or her own.

■ Step 4. Teach Vocabulary

Whether meant for children or for adult learners, things to be taught are usually presented in a graded order of difficulty, with easiest things first. Much work has been done in the reading field to determine the proper vocabulary and its order of presentation for teaching reading. This is the strong suit of most major series of traditional reading texts, which begin with a very few words in the first small book (just seventeen in some pre-primers) and gradually increase the vocabulary load. This increase in vocabulary can be seen on the last few pages of most children's reading texts. Such presentation can give teachers using this kind of basic series a built-in graduated vocabulary. Many teachers in the primary grades today use trade books and predictable books—ones that deliberately involve a lot of repetition—for beginning readers. (A Predictable Story, adapted for older developing readers, appears in the Step 2 Resources section of this book on page 22.)

However, when using programs designed for readers with underdeveloped skills, for individualized reading, and for literature-based reading programs, it is a good idea to supplement and cross-check normal vocabulary development and use a systematic list of new words to be taught. Such a list, the Instant Words, is discussed in the Step 4 Resources section that begins on page 50.

Instant Words

Here are the ten most frequently used words in the English language. If you can't read them, you can't read much. One of these words appears in almost every sentence.

the	in
of	is
and	you
a	that
to	it

The Instant Words are the most common words in the English language. They are arranged in order of frequency of occurrence in reading material and in the writing of new readers. To have ease in reading, students should learn to recognize these "sight" words instantly because they occur so very often. It is interesting to note that just the first 100 of these words make up almost one half of all reading material.

You can give your student the Instant Word Test on page 56 to find out which group of Instant Words to start teaching. Then you can teach them by having your student listen to them, review them, have spelling lessons on them, play card games with them, and so on. Several methods of teaching Instant Words appear in the Step 4 section of this book.

■ Step 5. Teach Basic Phonics

English is a phonetic language. This just means that letters and certain letter groups have regular speech sounds. There are plenty of exceptions to these patterns, but every good reader should know at least the basic principles of phonics. Phonics skills are a tremendous help to older students and adults in developing reading proficiency and are helpful also for spelling and using the dictionary.

Step 5 contains phonics charts with carefully chosen example words to help you teach the major rules of phonics. In addition, administering the Phonics Survey test (page 72) to each of your students will quickly reveal which basic phonics skills they know and those they need to work on.

For first-time readers as children, phonics instruction sometimes begins as reading readiness activities in kindergarten. Regular lessons in basic phonics skills usually start in the first grade, with the complete sweep of skills covered by third grade and reviewed and refined in later grades. In some parts of the United States, phonics is taught as part of a spelling program. Some teachers dislike formal or scheduled phonics lessons altogether, preferring instead to teach phonics as the need occurs. It makes little difference what you actually call phonics as long as your students learn the relationship between the letters and the sounds they stand for. As with teaching and improving reading skills, you start phonics instruction at the student's current level of development. Then you test, teach and review skills, test again, and teach some more.

Phonics Examples

The goal of phonics instruction is to help developing readers at every level learn the connection between letters or letter groups and the speech sounds they represent.

Similar Beginning Letter /k/	Similar Vowel Sound /ī/	Phonograms (Word Families) /-ĭt/
kind	five	bit
keep	ride	sit
kill	time	hit
key	like	fit

■ Step 6. Build Writing, Speaking, and Listening Skills

In years past, educators viewed reading and writing as two separate subjects. Today, however, it is not uncommon to have both reading and writing activities in the same lesson, at least some of the time. Literacy is, after all, defined as the ability to both read *and* write.

Step 6 will show you how to integrate both reading and writing into your lessons. It will provide you with suggestions for teaching writing fundamentals such as handwriting. It will also help you motivate students to write some of their own reading material, which can be a meaningful, creative outlet for them. You can also use students' own experience and language to develop stories, or Experience Charts. Students are motivated to create and read Experience Charts because they see their own words, which you have written down, about topics of special interest to them.

Students of any age readily see the usefulness of learning to write, whether they apply this valuable skill to activities at school, at work, or at home. And because language skills—reading, writing, speaking, and listening—are interrelated, a good teacher helps students to develop them all.

■ Trade Secrets

What follows are a few tricks of the teaching trade that educators have learned through their work in the Reading Center at Rutgers University. Although designed especially for children with underdeveloped reading skills, these ideas apply also to adult learners in basic education programs.

Success. Nothing motivates like success is the attitude taken at the Reading Center. A student should be successful with every lesson. If he or she is not, then the teacher or tutor has given the student the wrong lesson or has taught him in the wrong manner. The first challenge is to find the level at which he can be successful. If he can't read a whole sentence in an easy book, teach the student just one word and say, "That's great! We are really getting somewhere now. Let's see if we can learn two words today." By building a series of small success, you can gradually turn a reluctant reader into an engaged learner who looks forward to reading lessons.

Caring and Support. Older teens and adults who cannot read feel rejected by the world in many ways every day because of their low literacy skills. Many may feel like failures, cast aside and different from others. Not only have teachers failed to teach them, but teachers and society both constantly remind them of their problem just by giving the usual assignments in other subjects that involve reading, such as science or social studies, or by having written directions and newspapers around.

To be a successful reading teacher or tutor, you should try to alleviate as many aspects of this situation as possible. If love is too strong a word, let's say that you should empathize with your student's situation by being patient and understanding when working with him or her. You should care about the student and show it through words and deeds.

Ground Rules. Just as care and support suggest a certain warmth and allowance for personality differences, so setting a few ground rules suggest some structure for the teaching situation. You and your student are in this together, and you both have expectations for success. Your student should agree to come to lessons on time or call beforehand if he or she cannot attend, have a minimum of absences, not interrupt others, and complete homework assignments. There may be others that you agree on. If you work as a team within the framework of mutual respect, your teaching and the student's learning should go smoothly.

Interest. Most students are pretty poor actors when it comes to feigning interest. Learn to read the signs of boredom: losing the place in oral reading, being easily distracted, not showing up for lessons, and so on. The teacher must be skillful enough to present lessons that are easy enough to ensure success but difficult enough to provide challenge and growth.

Find out your student's interests and immediate goals of reading and gather a variety of reading material that reflects them. Besides stories and passages from instructional books, be sure to include practical items such as want ads for well-paying jobs, a drivers license training booklet, a timely sports column, or directions on a medication label. Also turn some practice exercises into competitive games, again keeping in mind that each student must experience some success.

Rewards. Most people have their behavior modified by rewards. How long would most people go to work if they were not paid? Even when we do things without being paid, we get a kind of reward: the satisfaction of helping others, enjoyment, companionship, or pleasure in doing something new. Sometimes a reward is delayed—most people attend classes to eventually find a job that will increase their earnings. But everyone enjoys receiving *some* immediate rewards, so the teacher or tutor should always be observant of a student's reactions and should offer a variety of rewards. Here are a few suggestions:

- Notice something at least once every lesson that your student has done well and give positive feedback for his or her good work.
- Keep a progress chart of new words learned and a portfolio of the student's work that demonstrates the progress he or she has made.
- See that the student has a chance to use newly acquired skills in a meaningful situation.
- Include in your lessons some activities or games that even poor students can feel successful with.

Fluency. Good readers and good writers seem to read with fluency almost effortlessly. They make it look easy. How did they achieve that skill? The answer is through repeated practice, just as experts at any skill, from playing tennis to playing the piano, must do to gain such proficiency. And even with some natural ability, most people need practice to develop a skill and added practice to improve it.

Students need to develop fluency, defined as "effortless reading with good comprehension." One effective way to do this is to give a lot of practice at an easy reading level before progressing to the next level of difficulty. Make sure the student has not only mastered a story or passage (reads it without errors and has good comprehension) but has much additional practice on the material before moving ahead. Progressing too quickly causes frustration, resulting in failure to learn and, sadly, dropping out of the reading program.

So far you've seen a one-sentence answer, a one-paragraph answer, and a one-chapter answer to the question of how to teach someone to read. With the information already given and with that presented in the succeeding chapters, you can teach any beginner to read and help a developing reader improve his or her skills.

Determine the Student's Reading Ability

The first step in teaching reading is to find out the current reading level of your student. There are few school students or adults in today's world who read nothing at all. Almost everyone has *some* reading ability. Where your student is concerned, your first job is to determine how much.

You may well be thinking that past instruction or inadequacies of the school system are really to blame for your student's underdeveloped reading skills, but the task at hand remains for you to find out what that student can read *right now*, before meaningful instruction can begin. When you succeed in teaching your student to read or to develop his skills well past the point where others left off, this older learner— whether young adult or middle-aged—will be ever grateful to you.

One quick and easy way to determine your student's current reading level is to administer the **Oral Reading Test.**

■ The Oral Reading Test

The purpose of this test is to aid instruction by determining your student's current reading ability. By having the student read aloud several paragraphs while you mark a different copy, you will learn his or her Independent Reading Level, Instructional Reading Level, and Frustration Level.

Independent Reading Level

The Independent Reading Level is that difficulty level of reading material at which the student can read with relative ease and independence; in other words, with little or no help from the instructor. The student should be able to pronounce nearly all the words in a passage at this level. You can give your student reading material at this level for pleasure, practice, and sustained silent reading.

Instructional Reading Level

The Instructional Reading Level is that difficulty level of reading material at which reading instruction is most effective. The student should know most of the words, not all. Use this level for instruction, such as oral reading or silent reading sessions, when you are around to help the student with difficult words.

Frustration Reading Level

Using material during reading instruction at too difficult a level (that is, with too many unknown words) slows the student's progress and can cause symptoms of tension and a dislike of reading to develop. Most of the time you should avoid giving your student reading material at his or her frustration level.

About Comprehension

The Oral Reading Test does not measure comprehension. At beginning reading levels, it is fairly safe to assume that comprehension roughly equals oral reading ability. However, reading comprehension and ways to measure it, discussed in Step 3, is not only essential, it is the whole point of reading and therefore well worth measuring on a regular basis.

Now turn to the Appendix on page 106, glance over the Oral Reading Test and directions, and administer it to your student.

STEP TWO

Select the Right Reading Material

You know how well your student can read if you have tested him or her with the Oral Reading Test. You also know the student's Independent and Instructional Reading Levels. Sometimes they are the same, but in any event, take care to avoid the Frustration Level.

Your next step is to find reading material at the right level for the student. Using the Readability Graph on page 13, you can find the reading level of any book, selection, or story. Using the less formal method of having the student read part of a selection orally and noting the number of errors made can also reveal whether the material in question is at the appropriate level.

Step 2 will also discuss instructional material and help you select the types appropriate to your student's interest and goals for reading.

■ Matching Student Skill with Material

Matching student reading ability with material at the correct difficulty level for a student is one of your most important jobs. If you give the student material that is too hard for her, she will become bored with it and may either stop reading it or read it with poor comprehension. Even struggling through the material will take her an excessive amount of time. On the other hand, if the student is given material that is too easy, which is not often the case, she may find it childish, again become bored, and stop reading.

Basic interest in the subject itself, of course, is an important motivation in the decision to read or to keep reading. As instructors discover, readability depends not only on such measurable items as sentence length, word length, and familiarity of words in a selection but also on the appeal of the content. A very high interest level can encourage a student to work through material more difficult than usual, compensating for a lack of proficiency at that level. However, just an average amount of interest will discourage the student at that same difficulty level and cause her to stop reading. Therefore, finding material that captures and holds the student's attention will go a long way toward getting her to read often, read widely, and thus broaden her general knowledge of the world.

Formal Matching

The Readability Graph will tell you the approximate difficulty level of any reading material. You can use it to match the student's reading ability (the grade level obtained from the Oral Reading Test) with the grade level of the material in question. Keep in mind that for reading instruction and especially for silent reading, it is better to use material a little too easy than a little too difficult. The reason is that reading easy material builds confidence in developing readers as they move right along without stumbling. Material a bit below level also promotes good comprehension instead of reading word by word or wordcalling.

Informal Matching

If you prefer not to use the Oral Reading Test or the Readability Graph as aids in selecting material, you can still match your student to material at the appropriate level by using the 1-error-in-20-words method. Simply choose a selection and ask him to read some of it aloud. If the student makes more than one mistake in every twenty words, the material is too hard for him, or is at his Frustration Reading Level. If he makes less than one mistake in every twenty words, the material is at his Independent Reading Level, and he should be able to read it silently with reasonable ease. If he makes about one mistake in every twenty words, the material is at his Instructional Level. Material at this level can be used in oral reading lessons or for silent reading when someone is close at hand to help him with difficult words. *Do not use material that is too difficult.* It blocks learning, frustrates the student, and makes your job more difficult.

Even if some educators have philosophical objections to testing students, it is good to remember that there are many approaches to teaching reading. However, occasional curriculum-based tests can be most effective in reinforcing lesson concepts for the student. This book also contains a variety of other teaching suggestions besides giving tests.

Interest Inventory

You need to learn about your students' interests, what things they read now, and what they want to do once they can read and write better. Their reading and writing goals can cover a broad range of necessary skills for daily living. They include

- **life skills:** Reading bills, menus, rental agreements, medication labels, bus/train schedules, cooking directions, neighborhood newsletters, voting materials and ballots, writing shopping lists, writing checks/balancing checkbook, filling out insurance/medical/unemployment forms, and applying for credit or for driver's license

Readability Graph

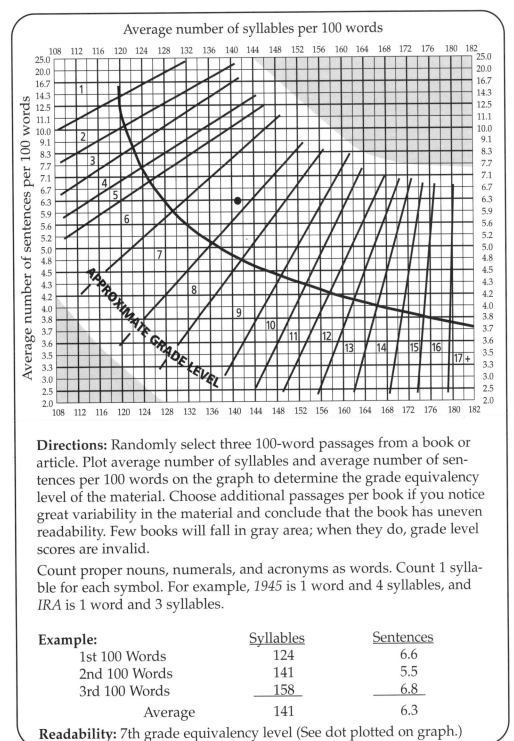

Average number of syllables per 100 words

Average number of sentences per 100 words

APPROXIMATE GRADE LEVEL

Directions: Randomly select three 100-word passages from a book or article. Plot average number of syllables and average number of sentences per 100 words on the graph to determine the grade equivalency level of the material. Choose additional passages per book if you notice great variability in the material and conclude that the book has uneven readability. Few books will fall in gray area; when they do, grade level scores are invalid.

Count proper nouns, numerals, and acronyms as words. Count 1 syllable for each symbol. For example, *1945* is 1 word and 4 syllables, and *IRA* is 1 word and 3 syllables.

Example:	Syllables	Sentences
1st 100 Words	124	6.6
2nd 100 Words	141	5.5
3rd 100 Words	158	6.8
Average	141	6.3

Readability: 7th grade equivalency level (See dot plotted on graph.)

- **job-related skills:** Reading want ads, job manuals, notes from co-workers, operating instructions, writing reports, filling out orders, or taking tests for jobs
- **educational pursuits:** Taking GED or other adult basic education classes, beginning a training program, and applying for college
- **parenting skills:** Reading to a child, reading notes and material from school, helping a child with homework, and writing notes or letters to school
- **reading/creative activities:** Reading for pleasure, reading the newspaper, checking out books or films from the library, doing crossword puzzles, and writing stories, poems, or keeping a journal

Use the Interest Inventory on page 19 at the end of this chapter as a guide. In an informal discussion, you can go through all or just parts of it with your student and record the responses. Or you can have copies of the inventory on hand and have the student fill it out if his or her writing skills are good enough. Filling out the inventory should be a pleasant experience, not a chore. Tell the student that not every item has to be answered, give help when needed, and don't be concerned about spelling and other errors.

You can then use the information from the inventory in selecting reading materials for lessons. Note that many of the inventory items can also serve as writing topics for the student later on.

■ Reading Materials

Materials appropriate for older and adult students to use for instructional reading and pleasure reading are different from such materials for children. **Trade books,** the term given to books published for the retail market, for both children and adults, are available in bookstores and libraries. Those for children include story classics like *Little Red Riding Hood* and *Winnie-the-Pooh,* as well as recently published books. However, trade books geared toward adult interests, such as classic novels, current bestsellers, and a broad range of nonfiction topics are, naturally, written at an adult reading level. These are likely to be too difficult for adult beginning and developing readers.

Fortunately, there are a number of resources available to help bridge the gap between low readability and adult interest.

Primary Resources

Many publishers carry supplemental educational materials, which are basic learning materials in the content areas of reading, writing and language, math, science, and social studies, written specifically for older and adult students. Many students use these materials in adult basic education programs to eventually earn a GED certificate, the equivalent of a high school diploma.

Publishers' catalogs may contain books and materials that cover the entire range of reading, writing, and language skills (and their assessment) from the literacy level through twelfth grade equivalency. Many fiction and nonfiction topics appropriate for your student may be listed under

- Reading and Comprehension
- Pleasure Reading
- Writing
- Spelling and Vocabulary
- Language Skills
- Study Skills
- Life Skills
- Family Literacy
- Workplace Skills
- Workplace Literacy

High-Interest Reading. Among the many materials for new and developing readers are those that deal with adult interests and concerns but are written at low readability levels (from 2.0 through 7.0 grade equivalency). These high-interest, lower-level books are often called **hi-lo** material, but most catalogs use the phrase "high-interest, low-level reading" when describing them. Written mainly for pleasure reading, hi-lo books can be fiction or nonfiction, are attractive and compact, and may have the look and feel of typical adult-level trade books. Like trade books, they offer characters, situations, and concerns appropriate for adult readers. They strive to be multicultural and avoid sexist and stereotypical issues.

Also available are standard literature classics, modern classics, and other quality fiction and nonfiction selections by contemporary authors adapted for low-level readability. In addition, a few publishers print easy-to-read newspapers that aim to simplify news and current events without sacrificing content.

Some hi-lo books are called **student readers**, designed to draw in reluctant readers. They most often contain short nonfiction selections on popular themes, current issues, and multicultural interests. Their readability level is typically from 2.0 through 6.0 or 7.0 grade equivalency. Hi-lo readers may have simple comprehension questions or short exercises in the book itself. These books often feature full-color art for visual interest and to give the student nonverbal comprehension clues. Instructional support typically consists of an activity-based teacher's guide and reproducible exercise sheets.

See Suggestions for Subject Matter in Step 3, page 28, for a summary of high-interest reading material arranged by subject matter.

Reading Programs. Quality reading material also appears in programs designed to teach basic reading and comprehension skills. These programs have graded student books with stories and exercises plus a separate teacher's guide for lessons and reading strategies using the material.

Some programs contain short, graded selections and have light instructional support. Other programs are broader in scope and include informational selections, adaptations of or excerpts from literature classics, drama, and poetry. These comprehensive programs have strong instructional support, such as step-by-step teacher guides and student workbooks, and can take adults and older teens from the beginning stages of reading to upper elementary levels.

Finding Suitable Materials. If you teach in a learning center, start your search within **your reading program**. The reading program should have a collection of high-interest, easy reading material or perhaps a list of books and their publishers. Also ask fellow teachers/tutors about locating other suitable material for your student.

The Adult New Reader section of **your local public library** contains high-interest low-level books including fiction, nonfiction, books on workplace skills and other supplemental books and materials from a variety of publishers. If your library doesn't have a special collection for adult beginning readers and those with underdeveloped skills, recommend that it start one. In the meantime, check the adult new reader collections at larger public libraries, such as regional libraries and city or town main libraries, which should have a fairly good selection of these materials.

Also ask the information librarian to help you find simple reading books in your student's interest area within the library's general collection.

Adult learning resource centers are community education agencies funded by the state (and some by the federal government). They offer libraries of low-readability materials, related resources, and workshops for teachers and tutors of older teen and adult developing readers.

Other Resources

Juvenile Trade Books. Not enough fiction and nonfiction reading books have been written specifically for the interests and concerns of adults with limited reading skills. After the hi-lo material available from the sources discussed above, however, the next best resource for students beyond beginning reading levels may be juvenile trade books. Some educators believe that these young adult trade titles (from about the sixth grade level and beyond), even when matched to the student's correct readability level, are inappropriate for older teens and adults, their content being too removed from adult situations and interests. However, juvenile books are still quality literature, and many older developing readers really like them. You might try reading a bit of a young adult book yourself to see if the content seems appropriate for your student. Remember also to look at the format of the book, any illustrations, and print size to make sure they don't look too childish. Better yet, if your student is with you at the library, look at some of these books together and go with what interests the student.

Also in the juvenile section are **student newspapers** that provide lower-level reading of current events, world news, multicultural stories, and other information of interest to your students. They may also contain crossword puzzles and other word games. Used copies of these newspapers are sometimes given away free by public schools.

Predictable Books. This special type of children's trade book contains a lot of repetition and for this reason is useful in teaching beginning reading to older and adult students as well as to children. These repetitious or "pattern" books give students practice (and success) in oral reading and add to their vocabulary. With teacher assistance, students might even enjoy creating and then reading predictable stories of their own based on everyday experiences. For an example of a predictable story adapted for adult beginning readers, see the sample story "Busy Day" and teaching suggestions at the end of this chapter on page 22.

An alternative to predictable stories is using **song lyrics** because they often have much repetition and because older learners may view them as more adult. Students can memorize the words and enjoy "reading" them with ease and success. See the end of this chapter for examples of song lyrics with repetition. Also encourage students to bring in lyrics to read, or have them use easy song patterns to make up lyrics of their own.

About Basal Readers. Children in school frequently learn to read from a set of books called a basal reading series, which contains stories and exercises for each grade level, usually 1 through 6. Traditional basal readers, like the old "Dick and Jane" series, were used successfully for decades to teach millions of children to read, but they later came under criticism for three main reasons.

1. The stories lacked high interest and good literary writing style.
2. The content of the stories was mostly about white, middle-class children from two-parent homes, a setting that hardly reflects contemporary family life.
3. The language used was considerably removed from the child's own language usage.

Basal readers published in recent years overcome many of these criticisms and can be useful in teaching reading to older learners as well as to children. However, aside from the serious drawback that often they seem childish to older students, these basal series also represent for many in this group the kind of material they failed as first-time readers. Understandably, these students have negative associations with such books.

It is up to you, based on the needs of your student, whether to use some books and materials from basal series for reading instruction. Public schools will sometimes lend or give you old copies of basal readers for the asking. In addition, many public libraries have some of them that they lend out free.

Because of the graded, systematic instruction of the books from beginning through the upper elementary levels and step-by-step teacher guides, a busy teacher or tutor can easily come to rely too heavily on these prepared materials. It is of utmost importance to balance the student's lessons with varied and relevant material, so if you do use basal readers, use them only in part; that is, select just a few stories from any single book to teach from. Avoid mechanically working through a series page by page, book by book.

Use the Library

- Introduce your student to the library and its services:

  Adult New Reader section   Reference section
  Ways to locate books   Videotapes
  Audiotapes   Job materials

- Help the student get a library card.
- Go through book check-out procedures together.
- Encourage the student to check out books often.
- Have the student read a bit of a book before bringing it home.

Real-Life Reading Materials

All reading material for older students and adults should be important and meaningful; these learners want practical knowledge and skills they can apply to their lives. Real-life, or environmental, materials are effective teaching tools for reading because they are readable, easily obtainable, interesting and fun to read, and can involve both reading and writing.

Below is a list of materials you can use for reading lessons. Be sure to consider any items on the student's interest inventory, and encourage students to bring in material as well. You might wish to reread the Interest Inventory section (pages 12–14) for a review of student reading and writing goals related to these real-life materials.

Everyday Life

Driver's license exam booklet
Signs: traffic-related, danger
Maps, bus/train schedules
Post office forms
Calendars
Credit/loan applications
Directions for assembling a toy
Emergency instructions
Using household cleaners
Care of clothing
Balancing a bank statement
Health/fitness pamphlet

Safety pamphlets
School notices
Report cards
Menus
Recipes
TV guides
Labels on food, medications
Sales flyers
Church bulletins
Travel brochures
Bills

General

Newspaper items: a human interest story, local news, a sports event, a health or fashion tip, a scientific discovery, advice columns, editorials, obituaries, horoscopes, classified ads, comic strips

Jokes: like ministories, they are short and will keep students reading for the punch line. (For some very funny jokes on universal themes, try the two-book set *Comedy Comes Clean, A Hilarious Collection of Wholesome Jokes, Quotes, and One-Liners* and *Comedy Comes Clean 2*, compiled by Adam Christing and published by Three Rivers Press, New York.)

Slogans on T-shirts, coffee mugs

Song lyrics

Employment

Job applications
Job ads
Instructions for operating equipment
Work reports

Orders/Requisitions
Unemployment forms
Employee benefit material
Office memos and notices

STEP 2 RESOURCES

Interest Inventory

Fill out a copy of this inventory with your student, or have the student fill it out and provide help when needed. The items are numbered so that if additional space is needed for some responses, the student can use the back of the sheet and refer to items by number.

Date _____

Student's Name _____

1. What do you do for a living? _____

   Where? _____

2. Describe briefly what you do on the job. _____

   _____

3. What do you need to read at work? _____

   _____

4. Would you like to do a different kind of work in the future? _____

   If so, what kind? _____

5. What further schooling or training might you do? _____

   _____

6. Do you have a hobby? _____ If so, what? _____

   _____

7. Do you like sports? _____ If so, which sports? _____

   _____

8. What would you do if you won a million dollars? _____

   _____

9. How do you like to relax? _____

_____

10. What do you do on vacation? _____

_____

11. If you moved, where would you like to live? _____

_____

12. What are your favorite kinds of food? _____

_____

13. What is your favorite TV show? _____

Favorite movie? _____

14. Check the items listed below that you read.

ITEM   READING FREQUENCY

	often	seldom	never
Job instructions			
Application forms			
Business letters			
Personal letters			
School notices			
Books to children			
Shopping lists			
Menus			
Television guides			
Catalogs			
Ads/junk mail			
Other			

15. Do you read the newspapers? _____ If so, what parts do you like to read?

_____

16. Do you read any magazines? _____ What kinds of magazines?

_____

17. Do you read any books? _____ What kinds of books?

_____

18. What would you like to read for pleasure? _____

_____

19. Check the items listed below that you write.

ITEM   WRITING FREQUENCY

	often	seldom	never
Business letters			
Notes at work			
Reports for work			
Personal notes			
Phone messages			
Notes to school			
Letters/cards			
Diary, log, journal			
Catalog orders			
Shopping lists			
Checks			
Other			

Predictable Story

Teaching Suggestions: Try this sample story with your beginning reader. He might have fun with it by reading it to a rhythm, such as a rap beat. Help the student to read this story several times. When he can read the story without much help, take words out of context or point to words at random and see if he can read them. Practice using many different words from the story, such as *work, teeth,* or *ate.* Then write some of the words on paper or the chalkboard, and see if he can still read them.

Busy Day

I got up in the morning and
    I brushed my teeth.
    I brushed my teeth.
    I brushed my teeth.

I brushed my teeth and
    I ate my breakfast.
    I ate my breakfast.
    I ate my breakfast.

I ate my my breakfast and
    I went to work.
    I went to work.
    I went to work.

I went to work and
    I did my job.
    I did my job.
    I did my job.

I did my job and
    I went home.
    I went home.
    I went home.

I went home and
    I played with my son.
    I played with my son.
    I played with my son.

I played with my son and
    I ate my dinner.
    I ate my dinner.
    I ate my dinner.

I ate my dinner and
    I went to class.
    I went to class.
    I went to class.

I went to class and
    I learned to read.
    I learned to read.
    I learned to read.

I learned to read and
    I learned to write.
    I learned to write.
    I learned to write.

I learned to write and
    I wrote my mom.
    I wrote my mom.
    I wrote my mom.

I wrote my mom and
    I wrote my friend.
    I wrote my friend.
    I wrote my friend.

I wrote my friend and
    I drove home.
    I drove home.
    I drove home.

I drove home and
    I watched TV.
    I watched TV.
    I watched TV.

I watched TV and
    I brushed my teeth.
    I brushed my teeth.
    I brushed my teeth.

I brushed my teeth and
    I went to bed.
    I went to bed.
    I went to bed.

What did I do today?
   I brushed my teeth.
   I ate my breakfast.
   I went to work.
   I did my job.
   I went home.
   I played with my son.
   I ate my dinner.
   I went to class.
   I learned to read.
   I learned to write.
   I wrote my mom.
   I wrote my friend.
   I drove home.
   I brushed my teeth.
   I went to bed.

And I'm tired
Because I've had
A busy, busy day.

Song Lyrics

Teaching suggestion: Words to songs are easy to memorize, but as with predictable stories, you should make sure that real reading is taking place. Remove some words from the song, write them in isolation on cards or on the chalkboard, or just point to them at random. Then see if your student can read the words out of context.

Sometimes I Feel Like a Motherless Child

Sometimes I feel like a motherless child,
Sometimes I feel like a motherless child,
Sometimes I feel like a motherless child,
A long ways from home,
A long ways from home.
True believer,
A long ways from home,
A long ways from home.

Sometimes I feel like I'm almost gone,
Sometimes I feel like I'm almost gone,
Sometimes I feel like I'm almost gone,
Way up in the heavenly land,
Way up in the heavenly land.
True believer,
Way up in the heavenly land,
Way up in the heavenly land.

Michael, Row the Boat Ashore

Michael, row the boat ashore, Hallelujah!
Michael, row the boat ashore, Hallelujah!

Brother, lend a helping hand, Hallelujah!
Brother, lend a helping hand, Hallelujah!

Sister, help to trim the sail, Hallelujah!
Sister, help to trim the sail, Hallelujah!

Jordan River is deep and wide, Hallelujah!
Meet my mother on on the other side, Hallelujah!

Jordan River is chilly and cold, Hallelujah!
Kills the body but not the soul, Hallelujah!

Trumpet sound the jubilee, Hallelujah!
Trumpet sound the jubilee, Hallelujah!

Michael, row the boat ashore, Hallelujah!
Michael, row the boat ashore, Hallelujah!

Lonesome Valley

You got to walk that lonesome valley.
You got to walk it by yourself.
For nobody else can walk it for you.
You got to walk it by yourself.

My Bonnie

My Bonnie lies over the ocean,
My Bonnie lies over the sea.
My Bonnie lies over the ocean,
Oh bring back my Bonnie to me.

Bring back, bring back,
Bring back my Bonnie to me, to me.
Bring back, bring back,
Oh bring back my Bonnie to me.

Yankee Doodle

1. Yankee Doodle came to town
    Just to ride the pony.
    Stuck a feather in his cap
    And called it *Macaroni.*

Chorus
    Yankee Doodle, keep it up.
    Yankee Doodle Dandy,
    Mind the music and the step,
    And with the girls be handy.

2. Fath'r and I went down to camp
    Along with Captain Good'in',
    And there we saw the men and boys
    As thick as hasty puddin'. (*Chorus*)

Typical **blues songs** are easy for students to read and even more fun to create. They can even use the familiar AAB pattern (two repeated lines plus rhyming last line) of these songs as a framework for making up their own blues.

Anybody's blues

A: You'll never miss the water till your well runs dry.
A: You'll never miss the water till your well run dry.
B: You'll never miss your honey till he says "Good-Bye."

Have the Student Read Aloud and Silently for Comprehension

Now that you have found your student's current reading level and matched it with the right reading material, the next step is getting the student to read as much and as often as possible. This includes both silent and oral reading for comprehension.

You should include both kinds of reading in a lesson. Many new and developing readers are embarrassed to read aloud, perhaps because of earlier negative experiences. If so, suggest that they do **silent reading** first. The material should be easy enough for reading with good comprehension. Also suggest that if they get to an unknown word, they skip it and keep on reading. Most often, they will get its meaning in context. It's OK to have them reread a passage several times until they feel comfortable with it.

Oral reading activities familiarize students with important style elements of a selection such as dialogue, humor, and various types of emphasis. It takes practice to develop fluency with it, but there are ways to ready students to read aloud. You can give them copies of the material and suggest that they follow the words and read silently as you read aloud. As they gradually build confidence in reading aloud, ask your student (or individual students) to read aloud as you (or other students) follow the reading. If students come to a word they stumble over as they read aloud, quietly give them the word and let them read on.

Choral reading, or reading as a group, can also help the student gain confidence in reading aloud because it doesn't call attention to the weakness of any one student. Again give out copies of the reading material so that all can follow along. You start reading and your student (or other students) join in the rest of the passage. Or, you and your student (or the group) can start reading aloud together, but you fade out and back in, which lets the individual or small group take the lead.

In teaching comprehension, **variety** is the key to adding interest to lessons and in keeping your student from getting bored with reading practice.

■ Vary the Subject Matter

Subject matter is one of the most obvious things that can and should be varied. It takes one approach to understand written instructions for operating equipment or baking a cake. It takes an entirely different approach to comprehend a short nonfiction selection or a story, and still another approach for a history lesson. All of these approaches involve reading, but helping the student identify the purpose for reading the material will directly affect the strategy you use. Is the student reading for pleasure, for information, to pass a test, or for some other purpose? You would want the student to read the history lesson more slowly and carefully than the story, and instructions even more carefully. You can teach students the differences in purpose through the kinds of questions you ask before, during, and after reading for each type of material you use.

Before discussing comprehension questions, here is a summary of the kinds of subject matter from which you and your students might draw for comprehension lessons and reading practice.

Suggestions for Subject Matter

Biography: Life stories of famous humanitarians (Albert Schweitzer, Mother Teresa), scientists and inventors (Thomas Edison, George Washington Carver, Madam Curie), artists and musicians (VanGogh, Mozart, the Beatles, Duke Ellington), political leaders, people who overcame tremendous odds, and even the lives of contemporary movie, TV, and rock stars

The Human Condition: Realistic fiction with contemporary adult themes and believable characters; stories that deal with family relationships, appreciating ethnic and racial diversity, and overcoming mental or physical illness; issues such as homelessness, spousal abuse, postwar trauma, alcoholism, and so on

Sports: Newspaper accounts of sports events; biographical sketches of famous sports figures; great moments in baseball, football, basketball

Mystery, Adventure/Survival, Romance, Science Fiction, and Modern Fantasy: Collections of interesting stories and easy trade-style novels by classic and contemporary writers

General: Short stories with surprise endings or other engaging plot twists

History: Historical events such as life in medieval times, wars, great inventions, natural disasters; can be nonfiction or historical fiction

How-to: Getting a job, following a recipe, staying healthy and fit, buying a car

Suggestions for Subject Matter *continued*

Humor: Jokes (Some are like ministories; students will want to get to the punchline.), anecdotes, quotations, comic strips

Little-known Facts: Compelling details and trivia to capture student interest and to create interest in topics the reader has not considered

Multicultural: Stories from around the world, global events, international selections about people, places, or things

Newspaper Items: Local news stories, scientific discovery, editorials, human interest stories, horoscopes, advice columns

Real-life Material: Drivers exam booklet, safety pamphlets, health or beauty tips

Traditional Stories: Folktales, fables, myths, legends, tall tales, such as "Aladdin's Lamp" and "Sinbad the Sailor"

■ Vary the Question Types

Good questions can help students experience reading comprehension as a thinking process that has general application to their reading outside of class.

The types of questions you ask students about what they are reading are important in helping them make sense of what is being read. And the more someone knows about a topic the more that person gets out of reading something about it, so choose a selection that students are likely to have some knowledge of. Before reading the text, they should look over the material and read titles, subheadings, and look at any illustrations that accompany the text. Ask students to share what they know about the topic and then to predict what they think the story or article will be about. In doing this they are integrating the subject matter and the purpose for reading with what they already know. It is at this point that you really see how the varied experiences and prior knowledge of older and adult learners can be used to their advantage.

Have the students read the first part of the selection, involving oral or silent reading, and then give clues from the reading that support or contradict their predictions. They can make new predictions about the next paragraph or section and continue reading. Continue this process, discussing content with students and asking them comprehension questions throughout the entire passage. If appropriate to the content, have the students react to the selection, using questions such as *What did you think about . . . ?* Have the students then summarize the reading, integrating new information with old.

Encourage students to keep in mind the time-honored "newspaper" questions—the *who, what, when, where, why,* and *how*—as they read. In moving through the selection with the students, avoid asking questions that can be answered yes or no or in one word; they are dead-end, cutting off further discussion. Open-ended questions such as *What would you have done in that situation?* or *What did the main character mean when he said, 'That woman is just asking for trouble?'* encourage discussion and reflection about the material.

The simplest type of question to ask is one about specific facts and details, such as *What color was the man's hair?* Recalling detail is an important literal comprehension skill, but you should also ask questions that check students' understanding of ideas not actually printed in the text. Some questions that call for these higher levels of thinking concern finding the main idea, awareness of time sequence (order of events), determining cause and effect, predicting events/outcome, summarizing, and drawing conclusions. A question such as the following asks students to read between the lines of a passage: *Fast food restaurants are described as serving food that only kids like that is loaded with salt, grease, and sugar. What do you think the writer wants us to think about the fast food industry?*

By using a variety of question types, you can hold student interest during the lesson and at the same time cover a wide range of comprehension skills. Don't ask questions that require comprehension skills above your student's level. Ask questions that he or she can often answer successfully.

Types of Questions

Setting

(*General*) Where does the story take place? (in the United States, in Europe, in the West, in New York City, in outer space?)

(*Specific*) Where does the story take place? (in a room, in a park, in a city, in the country?)

In what period of history does the story take place? (in the present, during World War II, in the Middle Ages, in prehistoric times?)

What do you know about that period from things you have heard or read?

Over what period of time does the story take place? (in a morning, a day, a year?)

What is the weather like? What does it have to do with how the characters felt or things that happened in the story?

Characters

Who would you say is the most important character? Why?

What kind of person do you think the main character is? Why?

Is this person happy? Honest? Explain your answer.

What does the main character look like?

What does he have to do with events in the story?

Types of Questions *continued*

Time Sequence

What happened first in the story?
What happened next?
What happened after . . . ?
When did the characters . . . ?

Summary

Restate the paragraph or story in your own words.

Main Idea

What is the selection mainly about?
What point is the writer trying to make?
What is the main idea of paragraph three? Is the main idea stated in
     a sentence in that paragraph? If so, which sentence is it?
What is the main idea of the whole selection?
Why did the writer choose this title for the selection?
Can you think of a better title?

Draw Conclusions (Conclusions must be supported by facts from the selection. A student responding to a *why* question should support his or her answer with a specific part or parts from the selection.)

How do you think the writer feels about . . . ? Why?
What can you conclude from the story about . . . ? Why?
Which of the following statements is probably true: . . . ? Why?
When the main character said, ". . . ," how do think he felt?
When the main character said, ". . . ," did he really mean something
     else? Give a reason for your answer.
What might happen next, if the story were to continue?

Newspaper Questions

Who? What? When? Where? Why? How?

Compare and Contrast

In this story, how are the main character and her sister alike?
How are they different? How do they change by the story's end?
Describe ____'s life before his wife died. Then describe ____'s life
     after his wife's death.
Of the two stories you read, which one was written longer ago?

■ Vary the Focus of Comprehension

In beginning reading, getting your student to read a single word or sentence is often a feat. But even after learning to read a whole paragraph, the traditional unit of meaning in teaching comprehension, your student should sometimes go back and focus on just one word, phrase, or sentence to clarify meaning. As his or her skills improve, you will no doubt use the standard technique of giving comprehension drills based on one or more paragraphs the student has read. As soon as possible, the student should read an entire selection and then a whole book, a feat which many students take real pride in accomplishing. Varying the focus of comprehension, ranging from the shortest unit of meaning (a word) to the longest (a book), can add a lot of interest to lessons on comprehension.

Comprehension questions about the various units of meaning can present an opportunity to deal with **idiomatic expressions** that may appear in some lesson material. Sometimes a developing reader, even one who is a native speaker of English, has trouble understanding a phrase or sentence that contains an idiomatic expression. An idiomatic expression is a group of words with a meaning different from what those words mean literally. For example, *It is raining cats and dogs* doesn't mean that cats and dogs are falling from the sky.

The literal meaning of many idiomatic expressions is easily pictured, which not only adds an element of humor to the explanation but also highlights the contrast between the literal and actual meaning of the idiom. However, to avoid comprehension problems, it is best not to give new or developing readers material containing idiomatic expressions, in independent reading material. If they must be included, make sure to discuss such expressions beforehand or check that a footnote explaining the expression appears on the same page. A list of common idiomatic expressions appears at the end of this chapter on page 37.

Remember to vary the focus of comprehension among the units of meaning contained in what the student is reading. Notice the amount of variety you can add to comprehension lessons by focusing on the different lengths of material.

Suggestions for Varying Units of Meaning

A Word

Getting the meaning of one word is often called vocabulary building, but it is also a kind of comprehension skill. Teachers should sometimes discuss a single word and ask questions about its meaning.

A Phrase

You should ask students about the meaning of certain phrases, for example one that is key in understanding part of a passage or story. You can also show how several words together (a phrase) may sometimes

Suggestions for Varying Units of Meaning *continued*

take on a meaning not contained in one word alone. For example, you might discuss the idiom *under the weather* and ask questions that lead students to understand that it doesn't have to do with weather but with feeling a bit ill.

A Sentence

You can use directed questioning to help students draw inferences from a sentence. Consider the sentence *As soon as the family reunion dinner was over, Denise left Milwaukee behind and headed for home.* Your questions about it might lead students to infer that Milwaukee is not Denise's home and maybe that family gathering was not a pleasant event for her.

A Paragraph

This is a traditional unit of meaning used to teach such skills as finding the main idea, locating supporting details, drawing conclusions, and understanding vocabulary in context. Although a useful length, a paragraph is one of several lengths of material to use in checking student comprehension.

A Chapter or Story

In many books, groups of paragraphs form a larger unit. Teach your students to read larger units; show that sometimes you have to see several paragraphs in relation to each other to get the meaning of a section. Ask questions that can be answered only by reading several consecutive paragraphs or the whole selection.

A Book

Even new readers sometimes enjoy long stories or selections. Guide them toward reading easy whole books, then ones slightly more difficult.

■ Vary the Difficulty Level of Material

The difficulty level of the material you choose for a student should vary. Naturally, you will give a lot of practice using easy material because it helps the reader feel successful, an especially important point when teaching older students and adults. Generally, these learners are afraid of failing (again) and may be easily discouraged, so efforts must be made to replace earlier unsuccessful, stressful reading experiences with successful ones. Since you do need to gradually move the student ahead to harder material, try out comprehension exercises first with easy material, then on material that is slightly more challenging. If the student experiences failure or frustration, return to the easy material for a while.

Attempting to vary the difficulty level of reading material helps maintain student interest in the reading process. In working with a particular student, you will learn when to give material below his or her reading level and when to nudge the student ahead with material just beyond the comfort level. Sometimes students may enjoy doing a comprehension exercise or reading a book that is very simple for them. Other times, however, they can feel absolutely triumphant about mastering material somewhat harder for them: the experience or prior knowledge students bring to a high-interest topic will help them use context clues and all reading skills they have to understand it. Therefore, take advantage of material that motivates learners to stretch their skills a bit.

■ Vary the Ways to Respond

As stated earlier, literal comprehension questions about facts and details are usually straightforward, requiring some recall of information in the reading materials. You ask a specific question and the student gives you a specific answer. It is important, however, to vary the *ways* in which students can respond to questions. You can specify in your questions or directions whether you want an **extended answer** (several sentences) or a **short answer** (a word or phrase), a **written answer** or a **verbal answer**.

The verbal/written option also applies to student responses to reading. An instructor might have students answer discussion questions verbally following silent reading one day and have the students silently read questions and write their responses following oral reading of a passage the next day.

Multiple-Choice Questions. Commercially prepared comprehension exercises often use multiple-choice questions. This question format is good not only for comprehension drills, it is frequently the one used to test students' knowledge in a wide variety of situations. Therefore, you should provide the student with guidance and practice in answering multiple-choice questions. A type of question similar to multiple choice but limited to two choices is the true/false question.

The Cloze Procedure. Another format to use for comprehension questions is the cloze procedure. It is sometimes called the sentence completion technique. Making cloze questions is very simple. Just knock out a word—any word—in a sentence and see if the student can fill it in and still make "sentence sense." The simplest kind of cloze procedure is that of mechanical deletion, in which you might, for example, just leave out every 10th word in a passage. Exercises designed to elicit more meaningful responses, such as filling in subject matter words (noun, adjective, verb, or adverb), can have spaces blank for only those words. Do not delete more often than every 10th word or the student will become a bit frustrated with the task. Some students, particularly those for whom English is a second language, need exercises on language usage. For these students, cloze techniques that knock out structure words (the kind of nonsubject "glue" words that hold sentences together) work well and hold students' interest. For example, a short cloze paragraph that offers practice with structure words might look like this:

Rosa went to _____ store for her mother.
"Are you the new girl in town?" asked the man _____ the store.

The student has to fill in the missing word. Take care to select passages for cloze exercises that are easy reading for the student.

Cloze is an excellent kind of exercise, but don't overuse it or the student will get bored. Remember to use the guideword of this chapter—variety—in finding different ways to test the same thing.

Student-Generated Questions. Questions are sometimes fun to make up. Simply ask your student to make up his or her own questions about a paragraph or a story using the methods discussed above. You should then answer the student's questions and both of you discuss the answers. If you have two or more students, they can pair off and make up questions for each other. Be sure to give the student positive feedback for making up the questions with something like, *That's a good question; it really made me think.* By commenting on what made the question good and by modeling good questions, you will notice that student questions improve each time you do this activity.

Retelling the Story. Retelling is a simple but very effective lesson in comprehension. Simply ask the student to retell the story in his or her own words after silently reading it. If a student cannot tell you the story, there is a good chance he or she has not understood it. If this happens, just ask the student to read the story again a bit more carefully because you are going to ask him to tell you all about it. This gives you the opportunity to clarify student comprehension by saying, *If there is any part of the reading that you do not understand, just ask me about it.* Incidentally, student retellings can be oral or written. Ask students with sufficient writing skills to write a short version of the story in their own words and provide them with help as needed.

Here is an excellent comprehension check to use with bilingual students. If the student's native language is Spanish, for example, and you speak it too, ask him or her to read the story in English but tell you about it in Spanish.

Summary of Response Modes

- Long and short answers, verbal and written ones
- Multiple choice or true/false
- Cloze method: student supplies missing word(s)
- Student-generated questions
- Retelling or summarizing the passage or story

■ Standardized Silent Reading Tests

Schools have traditionally given reading tests and made the scores available to parents, teachers, and tutors. Some important reading achievement tests are the California, Stanford, SRA, Metropolitan, and Iowa Reading Tests.

It is important to be somewhat familiar with silent reading tests. Formal or standardized tests tell you approximately what grade equivalency level of reading ability the student has achieved. These tests are important not just because they provide another useful measure (as do the oral tests) of a student's reading ability; they are useful also in measuring progress over the period of a year or more and in helping you select reading material at the appropriate difficulty level.

Not every section of a standardized silent reading test is equally valuable. The part that you should pay the most careful attention to is the one that measures paragraph comprehension. This section is sometimes called Comprehension or Reading Interpretation. Whatever its name, it consists of asking the student to read one or several paragraphs and then answer one or more questions about what he or she has just read.

A Reading Comprehension Test You Can Use

At some point, you may wish to test your student's reading comprehension. Although not required, it does give you some additional information about your student's reading ability.

In the Appendix on pages 114–124 are two reading comprehension tests you can use to measure the reading comprehension ability of an individual student or of a group. Test A is at approximately the third grade level; Test B is at approximately the seventh grade level. However, either test may be used with students of any age, including older and adult learners, to get some idea of their reading comprehension ability.

The items originated with the National Assessment of Educational Progress, which administered each item all across the United States. You can therefore compare your student's scores with the national norm for students reading at the equivalent of the third- and seventh-grade levels.

The items cover a variety of reading comprehension skills. Although you cannot conclude that a student is weak in a certain area based on one item alone, the items do indicate something about the student's abilities and do provide some suggestions for types of reading comprehension questions to use in drills.

Do not use the test items for teaching. You should not tell the student which items he or she got right or wrong, nor should you "go over" the test with the student. By doing so, you invalidate the use of the test for that student in the future. If you do not go over the test items with the student, that is, indicate which items are right or wrong, you can use exactly the same test at a later date to show progress in reading ability.

Step 2 (pages 14–18) describes the kind of material you can use to teach comprehension. The question types discussed on pages 29–31 will guide you in writing your own comprehension questions.

STEP 3 RESOURCE

Common Idiomatic Expressions

Below is a list of common idiomatic expressions used in American English. The first two idioms are stated, defined, and then placed in a real-life context to help students understand these expressions.

straight from the horse's mouth—(from a reliable source)

> How did you find out that Jill was engaged?
> I got the information **from a very reliable source.**
> You mean Jill told you so herself?
> That's right. I got it **straight from the horse's mouth!**

in the hole—(in great debt)

> Sadly, Sam had to sell his neighborhood hardware store. Because of competition from the bigger stores in the shopping center, he was going **in the hole** every month. His store was small and did not bring in enough income to meet expenses. As a result, Sam was rapidly **losing money and going into debt.**

He's **over the hill.**

I can't open this package—I'm **all thumbs.**

Time flies when you're having fun.

Dwayne is such **a wet blanket!**

He advised, **"If the shoe fits, wear it."**

Tell him to **go fly a kite.**

Linda's cousin **spilled the beans** about Jody's shower.

You just **put your foot in your mouth.**

The manager always **went to bat for me.**

Let's just **bury the hatchet** and be friends.

He **toots his own horn** about his talents.

You may disagree, but I'll make you **eat your words.**

I didn't mean to **blow up at** you. I'm sorry.

He couldn't **pull the wool over her eyes** this time.

He **fell for her.**

She **hit the ceiling** when she saw the bill.

The new show **brought down the house.**

His jokes **had me in stitches!**

She **turned a cold shoulder** to me.

You can **see right through him.**

His remark really **hit the nail on the head.**

Ed's ailing aunt is **on her last legs.**

The mayor went **out on a limb** for school reform.

Come on, you're **pulling my leg!**

Now you have to **face the music.**

Those two guys are **horsing around** instead of working.

Hey, grumpy, **what's eating you,** anyway?

I'll help you with math. That's **duck soup** for me.

After the new year, I will **turn over a new leaf.**

There is **something fishy going on** here.

We've got to **shake a leg** or we'll be late.

I'll tell you who won, but **keep it under your hat.**

Scott is feeling low. Yesterday he **got the ax** at work.

It's been a long day, so let's **hit the hay** early tonight.

Max asked me to **fork over** the ten dollars I owed him.

It really **turns me off** when Lee tries to talk with his mouth full.

The children **get in her hair** all the time, but she doesn't mind.

My uncle **feels like a million dollars** ever since his hip surgery.

Some people raved about it, but this movie is **for the birds!**

Laura kept **stringing Mark along** while she dated Tom.

I have to study hard for this exam—I don't want to **blow it.**

Dale, you haven't said a word all evening. What's the matter? **Cat got your tongue?**

Without proof of the extra hours I put in at work, I don't **have a leg to stand on.**

You have more skills than you take credit for. Don't **sell yourself short.**

The old man had money, but he **kicked the bucket** before telling where it was.

We know you're planning for Mom's next birthday. What do you have **up your sleeve?**

Look at my beautiful bedroom lamp! I got it **for a song** at a little shop.

They got a good price for the house they sold. Now they're really **sitting pretty.**

We don't have firm plans after the show. We can just **play it by ear.**

Things cost so much today that it's difficult to **make ends meet.**

Jan said she would help me clean house, but she **left me high and dry.**

Come on over to my house. We can have lunch and **shoot the breeze.**

James is recovering nicely from the accident, but he's not **out of the woods** yet.

A rush job just came in. We have to put our project **on ice** for now.

This theater has really **gone to the dogs.** It used to be beautiful.

Teach Vocabulary

Reading teachers usually divide the job of teaching vocabulary into two distinct levels. The first is teaching a **basic sight vocabulary** of common words that beginning readers must master. The second level involves building upon that groundwork by learning the meaning of new words, or **vocabulary building**. This chapter will show you first how to determine which basic sight words your students already know and present some methods for teaching these words. Then it will discuss vocabulary-building techniques for students reading beyond the third-grade equivalency level.

■ Basic Sight Vocabulary

Beginning readers, defined as anyone (of any age) whose ability ranges from none to the upper third-grade equivalency level, need to master a high-frequency vocabulary, such as the Instant Word list at the end of this chapter (pages 50–55). The students should be able to read the first 300 of these words "instantly"—without a moment's hesitation—because these words make up about 65 percent of all written material. That is, more than half of the text of every newspaper article, textbook, new adult reading book, and novel is composed of just these 300 words. You can scarcely write a sentence without using several of them, for they are the "glue" words that hold sentences together and appear over and over again. Moreover, it is virtually impossible for students to concentrate on comprehension if they are stuck on a word such as *their*.

Another problem is that some of these high-frequency words are irregular and do not follow phonics rules well. For example, how does a student sound out *of* or *said*? The answer is that beginning readers need to learn these words as "sight words," common words immediately readable by students when they see them.

Testing the Instant Words

A basic tool for every teacher of beginning and developing readers should be a list of the words most frequently used in English. Both first-time readers and those with underdeveloped skills from previous instruction often have spotty reading vocabularies. They know some relatively uncommon words but do not know certain high-frequency basic words.

Most basic reading textbooks (basal readers) have a graded word list built into the series. Many students, however, may not have followed such a series or may have learned only part of the word list. Whatever the reading history, it is important to "find out where the learner is."

To do this with individual students is easy. Give them the **Instant Word Test** on pages 56–57 or simply ask them to read aloud from each column of the Instant Words (pages 50–55). Then stop and teach them the words they don't know.

In a group setting, a good way to assess word knowledge for beginning readers is to make a recognition test. Duplicate a group of Instant Words, four words per line, and number the lines. Give each student a sheet of the words and then say, "On line one, put an X on the word *you*; on line two, put an X on the word *that*," and so on.

The test results will help you easily group pupils by ability. Save the students' tests for word review at a later time.

Instead of using this survey test, you may simply have students read every word on the Instant Word list—but not all at once. Have them learn a column or part of a column at each lesson, until they have accumulated enough unfamiliar words for the day's lesson.

Teaching the Instant Words

Since a high percentage of all reading material is composed of relatively few words, learning to read would appear to be a task that is ridiculously easy. If 300 words will do most of the job, why not begin with just these words, teach them quickly, and move on to the next level? The answer is that the learning experience is more complex than that.

Experience has shown that mastery of the first 300 Instant Words, or any basic vocabulary list of this size, normally takes about three years for first-time beginning readers. An average child in an average learning situation knows most of the first 100 words by the end of the first year of instruction. The second 100 words are added during the second year. It is not until some time during the third year that all 300 words are really mastered and used as part of the student's reading vocabulary. This is not to deny that students at the second and third grade reading levels can "read" many more words than the 300 Instant Words. They can also read many proper nouns and a smattering of subject words related to the type of material that they have encountered.

Teachers can expect to decrease the learning time required to teach older and adult students in programs for new and developing readers. Nevertheless, students' mastery of the first 300 Instant Words closely parallels the students' reading level attained thus far. For example, a person who can just manage to read material at the upper second-grade reading level barely knows most of the first 200 Instant Words.

A list of 600 Instant Words appears at the end of this chapter. The words are ranked in order of frequency, with the most common words first. It is important that beginning students know most of the first 300 of these words "instantly" before proceeding to the remaining 300 words, which should be included in reading and spelling lessons with students at about the fourth- and fifth-grade reading equivalency levels.

Methods for teaching the Instant Words will vary with the teacher, the student, and the learning situation. Any method that works is a good one, but note that the Instant Words are presented in groups of five to discourage instructors from teaching too many words at one time. The rank order of the list is also the suggested teaching order in which beginning readers normally learn new basic words while they learn many other terms, such as names or subject words. Some students can learn only two or three words per week, and others can master twenty with ease. Both groups, however, need frequent word review.

Suggested activities include plenty of easy reading practice, use of flash cards, card games, and spelling lessons augmented by a lot of positive feedback and encouragement. Activities that also involve competition are fun and help hold the students' interest. Whether teaching students one-on-one or in a group setting, the important message for teachers to convey to students, by both word and deed, is that they care about them, that they want them to be able to read, and that learning these Instant Words is important.

Easy Reading Practice. Easy reading practice is one of the best ways of teaching the Instant Words. Easy reading material is printed matter in which a student can pronounce 99 percent of the words or, using another rule of thumb, material in which a student averages fewer than one mistake for every 20 words. For a student who can read at the second-grade equivalency level, whether with help or hesitatingly, easy reading is material written at the first-grade level. For a student reading at the sixth-grade equivalency level, easy reading is material at the fourth- or fifth-grade reading level. Easy reading is important because each reading that students attempt gives them a feeling of success and encourages them to learn new words. And because easy reading practice is certain to contain the Instant Words, students who barely know these words get a lot of practice in recognizing them. In addition, easy reading practice also helps students learn to apply context clues in making sense of what they read.

Easy reading, therefore, is reading that is a grade or two below where the student *can* read. It is no accident that most popular novels are written at about the eighth-grade difficulty level and that most book buyers are at least high school graduates.

Flash Cards. Many teachers and tutors use flash cards for sight word reading. A **flash card** is simply a card with a word written on it. The word is written in bold print and, usually, in lowercase using a marker. By cutting off the upper right hand corner of the card, the printed word will always be right side up and facing the person who restacks the cards.

A traditional way to teach with flash cards is to choose a small number of words, such as five Instant Words. Tell the student each word and briefly discuss it, perhaps using it in an oral sentence. Next, mix up the cards and "flash" them to the student while he or she tries to quickly call out the word. If the student misses, tell him the word. (Don't use phonics at this point.) Mix up the words and flash them to the student again. When the student knows all the words, put the cards away and, at the next lesson, review the words by flashing the cards again and helping the student with any words missed.

Flash cards also make great review lessons, and students often need considerable review of words learned. Just because they have mastered a list one day doesn't necessarily mean that they will remember all of the words the following week. Never blame students for forgetting, but applaud them for any words remembered and patiently teach the words missed. Everyone needs repetition in learning something new, whether it's new words, people's names, unfamiliar terms of a particular business, or a foreign language.

It is also a good idea to display flash cards and refer to them at times other than during a word review itself. Teachers can line them up on the chalkboard for reference while the group does a different reading activity, and tutors might give a small stack of cards to a student for practice at home.

Flash cards are also effective as sentence builders. Arrange two or three or more flash cards so that they make a phrase or sentence. Some interesting sentences can be made using **rebuses,** which are simply pictures used in place of words, as in the following example:

The  hit the  .

Read this as *The man hit the dog.*

The teacher can also use flash cards in games with a small group of students, flashing each word as quickly as possible. The student who says the word first holds that card. The point of the game is to see who gets the most cards. Give each student a turn at recognizing the word; when one student misses, the next one gets the turn.

Students might sometimes work alone with a small pack of flash cards, separating them into two piles: the words they know and those they do not know. When the students are finished, the teacher or a student who knows the words checks the "know" pile and then helps individual students with words in the "don't know" pile.

You (or your students) can make flash cards using blank calling cards (obtained from a local printer), index cards, or even scraps of paper. Copy the entire word list to be learned or make cards only for words that students miss when reading through the list.

Teaching Tip

Remember that teaching only a few words at a time keeps the student's success rate high.

Games. Bingo is an excellent game for teaching the Instant Words in a group setting or one-on-one. Place twenty-five words (in five rows and five columns) in random order on a card, with a card for each player. Each player's card contains the same words but arranged in a different order. The teacher or tutor calls off the words in random order or draws word cards out of a box or hat. Markers can be small cardboard squares, beans, bottle caps, or anything handy. The first student to complete a row, column, or diagonal line wins.

Often, even after there has been a winner, students like to keep playing until the cards are filled and every word is covered. Playing the game this way helps the teacher spot poor readers by observing the number of uncovered words on students' cards. A situation in which some of the students do not know all of the words is a great opportunity for the teacher to introduce an unfamiliar word by writing it on the board after saying it. Playing until all cards are covered also gives poor readers an equal chance at winning.

Note that a set of twenty-five words will fit on a card with five rows and five columns. For beginning readers, however, having just nine words (in three rows and three columns} on a card may be enough.

Sample Bingo Card

the	of	it	with	at
a	can	on	are	this
is	will	you	to	and
your	that	we	as	but
be	in	not	for	have

Pairs is another game played with great success. Pairs is played like rummy or Fish in that only two cards are needed to make a pair. Two to five persons may play. Five word cards are dealt to each player, and the remainder of the deck is placed in the center of the table.

The object of the game is to get as many pairs as possible. Each deck has sets of two identical cards.

The player to the right of the dealer may ask any other player for a specific card, for example, "Do you have *are*?" The player who asks must hold the mate to the *are* card. The player who is asked must give up the card if he or she holds it. If the first player does not get the card he asks for, he draws a card from the pile. Then the next player takes a turn to ask for a card.

If the player succeeds in getting the card he asks for, either from another player or from the pile, he gets another turn. As soon as the player gets a pair, he puts it down in front of him or her. The player with the most pairs at the end of the game wins.

If the player *doing the asking* cannot read the word on the card, he may show the card and ask any of the other players or anyone present.

If the player *who is asked* for a card cannot read that word or is unsure of it, he should ask to see the card of the player requesting the card or ask a nonplaying reader to look at his cards.

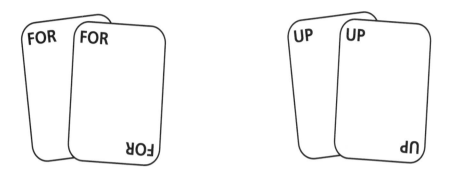

Make two cards for each word used in a Pairs deck.

Make the word cards for Pairs decks using a group of twenty-five Instant Words. Two cards for each word makes a fifty-card deck. Teachers or students themselves can make the cards, which should contain words at the appropriate level of difficulty for the students. Although it is good for students to periodically review easy words already mastered, instructional games should generally follow the same rules as those used to select instructional reading material—the words used for the games should be not too easy and not too hard. The students, therefore, should know some but not all of the words used in a particular deck. They should have help in playing until they know almost all of the words and can get along by themselves. This level of mastery is usually attained quickly because students like the game.

The students should play the game several times until they can call out all the words instantly. They should then progress to a deck of word cards at the next level of difficulty, periodically reviewing words from easier decks.

Concentration™ is another game that can be played using a Pairs deck. Spread a deck of fifty cards facedown on a table in mixed order. One to four players take turns drawing two cards at random. If the cards drawn are not a pair, the player puts them back in exactly the same place, facedown. The trick of the game is to remember card location in order to make a pair with each two cards turned up. From an instructional standpoint, the student gets practice in reading aloud each card turned over. If a player taking a turn doesn't know how to read the card, another player can help by saying the words.

Spelling. The Instant Words may be used for spelling lessons, especially those words that students have trouble learning to read. However, the Instant Words are just as important for student writing as they are for reading because students need basic structural words such as *and, to,* and *is* to hold sentences together. A typical spelling lesson has the following elements:

1. Put the words for the student to learn on a chalkboard, a sheet of paper, or on flash cards. Have the student read them aloud, sometimes using them in a sentence for you so that you are sure he knows how to pronounce them and understands their meaning.

2. Have the student copy the word list or write sentences using the words.

3. Give the student a trial test, which means that the teacher says each word and the student tries to write it.

4. Correct the student's test, circling incorrect letters and supplying missing letters.

5. Have the student study the spelling errors and write the word correctly, perhaps a few times. (See the five-step study method below.)

6. Give the student a final test. Add any words the student misses to the spelling list for the next class or session.

It is important to avoid presenting too many words in a spelling lesson. Five to ten words are enough for a student reading at the first-grade equivalency level, and twenty words are enough for those at reading levels three through six.

Five-Step Spelling Method for Students

1. **Look** at the whole word carefully.
2. **Say** the word aloud to yourself.
3. **Spell** each letter aloud to yourself.
4. **Write** the word from memory. (Cover the word and write it.)
5. **Check** your written word against the correct spelling. (Circle errors and repeat Steps 4 and 5.)

Picture Nouns. At the end of this chapter is a list of 100 words, called **picture nouns,** intended to supplement the Instant Words. The list of Instant Words does not contain many "subject words," or words that describe content. New readers need to know some easily pictured nouns—name words, like *car* or *letter*—to read and write sentences and short personal experiences.

car

boat

You can teach a group of five picture nouns along with the Instant Words, which are also presented in groups of five words. Picture nouns are particularly useful when using flash cards to build sentences because you can use the picture side of the card as a rebus (a picture for a word in a sentence).

Picture nouns can also be used to improve thinking skills. Simply mix up two or more groups of five picture nouns and have students sort them into categories of things that belong together. This activity fosters organizational skills while giving students practice reading common words they use every day.

The picture nouns can also be used in simple self-teaching lessons. Give the student a stack of cards with the word side facing up. The student tries to read the word, and if he can't, he turns the card over and looks at the picture.

Most of the games and techniques used in teaching the Instant Words can also be used with the picture nouns.

■ Vocabulary Building

Educators usually use the term **vocabulary building** in connection with students who are reading beyond third grade difficulty level. More specifically, these are students who can recognize instantly most of the first 300 Instant Words and who have an adequate grasp of basic phonics skills. They are ready to build on the groundwork of their basic sight vocabulary and, because they are likely not first-time readers, will once again use their wealth of prior knowledge and life experience to their advantage, this time on the vocabulary front.

Even if not done consciously, people (both good readers and poor ones) are always adding new words to their vocabulary by virtue of living in a society bombarded by language from all media. Your students, who have taken the initiative to improve their reading and language skills through a reading class or tutoring sessions, will be receptive to the following ways to step up their rate of vocabulary growth.

Notice New Words

Encourage your students to pay attention to new words. Help students develop the habit of noticing new words. When they encounter a new word while reading, they should *pause and pay attention to it.* You should explain how students might go about getting the meaning of an unfamiliar word from its context (the way it is used in the sentence). If they don't know the meaning of the word after using context clues, they should write it down on a separate sheet of paper or in a notebook for later use. In the meantime, it's okay to ask someone the meaning of the word or "ask" the dictionary.

Use Direct Instruction

Another way to help students expand their vocabulary is through direct instruction. Although getting meaning of a word from context often happens naturally, especially when that word is nestled within the text of a book that's almost impossible to put down, it is still important to present proven methods of learning new words.

Teaching the Meaning of Words. Some teachers and tutors introduce a new word or words at each reading lesson by writing them on the chalkboard, using flipcharts or bulletin boards, or placing word cards on the table and then briefly discussing the words. For example, you might write down and talk about the word *inclement* on a rainy day, or *torrid* on a real scorcher. Or maybe the student picks up a new word, such as *seismograph,* from a TV or radio report, in conversation, or from a newspaper article about earthquakes.

Working with Prefixes, Roots, and Suffixes. Students can have many new words at their command if they learn how to use prefixes, roots, and suffixes to form new words. Even children know that the **prefix** *un-* in front of a base word changes its meaning, as in *unhappy*, and that they can extend this principle to learn the meaning of *unable*. The same idea applies to word parts called **roots,** which come from Latin and Greek words. For example, the root *tele-* means "far," so *telescope* means "seeing something that is far away." This root is also found in *television, telegram,* and so on, and helps to explain the meaning of those words. **Suffixes** are word parts added to the ends of base words. For example, the suffix *-er* added to the base word *sing* changes its meaning to "one who sings."

A list of common prefixes, roots, and suffixes appears at the end of this chapter as a ready reference to use when teaching them. In addition, most large dictionaries give the root meaning of many words, information that helps students learn the meaning of a particular word as well as others containing that root. When teaching the use of prefixes, roots, and suffixes, take the time to also teach or review basic dictionary skills.

Use New Words

Finally, keep in mind that learning new words is a lifelong task for your student and for you too. Each time you start to learn about a new subject or read a new book, you encounter new words to learn. Welcome the opportunity and enjoy it. Help students make a new word they've seen or heard "their own" by encouraging them to use these words in their speech and writing. Give positive feedback when they do, even if they mispronounce or misspell the words, because it is mainly through use that new words become a permanent part of vocabulary.

Vocabulary Building—Summary

Teach Students to
1. Pay attention to a new word encountered.
2. Try to learn its meaning from context.
3. Ask someone the meaning of the new word.
4. Look it up in a dictionary.
5. Learn a new word each day.
6. Use prefixes, roots, and suffixes to expand vocabulary.
7. Use new words often.

STEP 4 RESOURCES

600 Instant Words

These are the most frequently used words for reading and writing, listed in rank order. These high frequency words are also called *sight words* because students must recognize them instantly on sight to gain reading fluency. Columns 1–4 contain the first 100 words. Make sure your student knows most of them before teaching the second 100. Teach only a few words at a time to keep the student's success rate high.

The First Hundred Instant Words

Column 1 1–25	Column 2 26–50	Column 3 51–75	Column 4 76–100
the	or	will	number
of	one	up	no
and	had	other	way
a	by	about	could
to	word	out	people
in	but	many	my
is	not	then	than
you	what	them	first
that	all	these	water
it	were	so	been
he	we	some	call
was	when	her	who
for	your	would	oil
on	can	make	now
are	said	like	find
as	there	him	long
with	use	into	down
his	an	time	day
they	each	has	did
I	which	look	get
at	she	two	come
be	do	more	made
this	how	write	may
have	their	go	part
from	if	see	over

600 Instant Words *continued*

The Second Hundred Instant Words

Column 5 101–125	Column 6 126–150	Column 7 151–175	Column 8 176–200
new	great	put	kind
sound	where	end	hand
take	help	does	picture
only	through	another	again
little	much	well	change
work	before	large	off
know	line	must	play
place	right	big	spell
year	too	even	air
live	mean	such	away
me	old	because	animal
back	any	turn	house
give	same	here	point
most	tell	why	page
very	boy	ask	letter
after	following	went	mother
thing	came	men	answer
our	want	read	found
just	show	need	study
name	also	land	still
good	around	different	learn
sentence	form	home	should
man	three	us	America
think	small	move	world
say	set	try	high

600 Instant Words *continued*
The Third Hundred Instant Words

Column 9 201–225	Column 10 226–250	Column 11 251–275	Column 12 276–300
every	left	until	idea
near	don't	children	enough
add	few	side	eat
food	while	feet	face
between	along	car	watch
own	might	mile	far
below	close	night	Indian
country	something	walk	real
plant	seem	white	almost
last	next	sea	let
school	hard	began	above
father	open	grow	girl
keep	example	took	sometimes
tree	beginning	river	mountain
never	life	four	cut
start	always	carry	young
city	those	state	talk
earth	both	once	soon
eye	paper	book	list
light	together	hear	song
thought	got	stop	being
head	group	without	leave
under	often	second	family
story	run	later	it's
saw	important	miss	afternoon

600 Instant Words *continued*

The Fourth Hundred Instant Words

Column 13 301–325	Column 14 326–350	Column 15 351–375	Column 16 376–400
body	order	listen	farm
music	red	wind	pulled
color	door	rock	draw
stand	sure	space	voice
sun	become	covered	seen
questions	top	fast	cold
fish	ship	several	cried
area	across	hold	plan
mark	today	himself	notice
dog	during	toward	south
horse	short	five	sing
birds	better	step	war
problem	best	morning	ground
complete	however	passed	fall
room	low	vowel	king
knew	hours	true	town
since	black	hundred	I'll
ever	products	against	unit
piece	happened	pattern	figure
told	whole	numeral	certain
usually	measure	table	field
didn't	remember	north	travel
friends	early	slowly	wood
easy	waves	money	fire
heard	reached	map	upon

600 Instant Words *continued*

The Fifth Hundred Instant Words

Column 17 401–425	Column 18 426–450	Column 19 451–475	Column 20 476–500
done	decided	plane	filled
English	contain	system	heat
road	course	behind	full
half	surface	ran	hot
ten	produce	round	check
fly	building	boat	object
gave	ocean	game	am
box	class	force	rule
finally	note	brought	among
wait	nothing	understand	noun
correct	rest	warm	power
oh	carefully	common	cannot
quickly	scientists	bring	able
person	inside	explain	six
became	wheels	dry	size
shown	stay	though	dark
minutes	green	language	ball
strong	known	shape	material
verb	island	deep	special
stars	week	thousands	heavy
front	less	yes	fine
feel	machine	clear	pair
fact	base	equation	circle
inches	ago	yet	include
street	stood	government	built

600 Instant Words *continued*

The Sixth Hundred Instant Words

Column 21 501–525	Column 22 526–550	Column 23 551–575	Column 24 576–600
can't	picked	legs	beside
matter	simple	sat	gone
square	cells	main	sky
syllables	paint	winter	glass
perhaps	mind	wide	million
bill	love	written	west
felt	cause	length	lay
suddenly	rain	reason	weather
test	exercise	kept	root
direction	eggs	interest	instruments
center	train	arms	meet
farmers	blue	brother	third
ready	wish	race	months
anything	drop	present	paragraph
divided	developed	beautiful	raised
general	window	store	represent
energy	difference	job	soft
subject	distance	edge	whether
Europe	heart	past	clothes
moon	sit	sign	flowers
region	sum	record	shall
return	summer	finished	teacher
believe	wall	discovered	held
dance	forest	wild	describe
members	probably	happy	drive

If you want additional Instant Words for reading or spelling lessons, the entire list of 3000 Instant Words can be found in the *Spelling Book, Words Most Needed Plus Phonics for Grades 1–6*, by Edward Fry, available from Teacher Created Materials (800/622-4321).

Instant Word Test

The Instant Word Test is located on the next page. Ask individual students to read each word aloud slowly. Use a copy of the Instant Word Test for scoring, placing a C next to each word the student reads correctly. Allow for differences in regional dialects, but accept only meaningful pronunciations. Do not give the student any help; if the student does not know a word after five seconds, tell him or her to go on to the next word.

Discontinue the exam when a student misses five words, not necessarily in consecutive order. Find the last correct word before the fifth error and multiply its position number by 15 to get the student's *approximate* instructional placement.

Because it is not standardized, the test does not yield a grade level score. It can, however, be used to determine where to begin working with a student on the first 600 Instant Words. Do not use the test for teaching; use the complete list of 600 Instant Words.

Instant Word Test

Date _____

Student's Name _____

Directions: Student reads aloud from one copy and examiner marks another copy. Stop after the student misses five words. Do not help the student. If the student makes an error or hesitates five seconds, say, "Try the next word."

Scoring:
( ) Position number of last correct word before the fifth word missed
x 15
( ) Approximate placement on the first 600 Instant Words list

For example, if the last correct word was 10 on the list below, then 10 x 15 = 150. You would then start teaching the Instant Words with word 151 in Column 7.

Test for the First 300 Words (approximately every 15th word in the First 300 words)	**Test for the Second 300 Words** (approximately every 15th word in the Second 300 words)
1. are	21. room
2. but	22. become
3. which	23. whole
4. so	24. toward
5. see	25. map
6. now	26. king
7. only	27. certain
8. just	28. stars
9. too	29. nothing
10. small	30. stood
11. why	31. bring
12. again	32. check
13. study	33. heavy
14. last	34. direction
15. story	35. picked
16. beginning	36. window
17. feet	37. wide
18. book	38. sign
19. almost	39. root
20. family	40. describe

100 Picture Nouns

The name words listed below are intended to supplement the first 300 Instant Words so that beginning and developing readers have the basic words they need to read and write sentences and paragraphs. You can make flash cards to teach these words, placing a word on one side only, or make cards with a word on one side and its picture on the other.

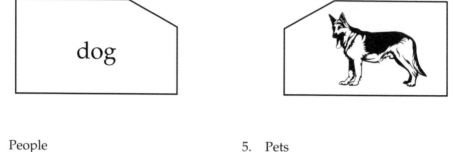

1. People
    boy
    girl
    man
    woman
    baby

2. Tools
    hammer
    broom
    saw
    shovel
    mop

3. Numbers 1–5
    one
    two
    three
    four
    five

4. Clothing
    shirt
    pants
    dress
    shoes
    hat

5. Pets
    cat
    dog
    bird
    fish
    rabbit

6. Furniture
    table
    chair
    sofa
    chest
    desk

7. Eating Objects
    cup
    plate
    bowl
    fork
    spoon

8. Transportation
    car
    truck
    bus
    plane
    boat

100 Picture Nouns   *continued*

9. Food
   bread
   meat
   soup
   egg
   cereal

10. Drinks
    water
    milk
    juice
    soda
    tea

11. Numbers 6–10
    six
    seven
    eight
    nine
    ten

12. Fruit
    apple
    orange
    grape
    pear
    banana

13. Plants
    bush
    flower
    grass
    plant
    tree

14. Sky Things
    sun
    moon
    star
    cloud
    rain

15. Earth Things
    lake
    rock
    dirt
    field
    hill

16. Farm Animals
    horse
    cow
    pig
    chicken
    duck

17. Workers
    farmer
    policeman
    cook
    doctor
    teacher

18. Entertainment
    television
    radio
    movie
    baseball
    band

19. Writing Tools
    pen
    pencil
    crayon
    chalk
    computer

20. Things to Read
    book
    newspaper
    magazine
    sign
    letter

Prefixes

Prefixes that Change a Word's Meaning to its Opposite

Prefix	Meaning	Example
anti-	against	antiwar, antidote, antisocial, antislavery
dis-	not, away from	disagree, dishonest, disable, displease
mis-	wrong	misplace, misconduct, misfortune, misspell, misbehave
non-	not	nonsense, nonsmoker, nonviolent, nontoxic, nonverbal
ir-	not	irresponsible, irreversible, irreparable
il-	not	illegal, illegible, illegitimate, illogical
im-	not	impossible, imbalance, immature, immobile
in-	not	incorrect, incapable, inconsiderate
un-	not	unkind, unable, unhappy, uncertain, unbeaten, uncomfortable, unhealthy

Prefixes that Show Time

Prefix	Meaning	Example
ante-	before	antecedent, anteroom, antedate
pre-	before	prepare, prenatal, prejudice, predict, precaution, prefix
post-	after	postpone, postwar, postmortem, postoperative, postgraduate

Prefixes that Show Place

Prefix	Meaning	Example
de-	down, away	descend, detract, degrade, defrost
in-, en-	in, inside	interior, insure, enclose, enfold
ex-	out	external, exit, extract, exponent
sub-	under, below	submarine, subzero, subterranean
super-	above, over	superhuman, supernatural, superstar, supervisor, superintendent, superpower
pro-	forward	proceed, promote, propose, propel
trans-	across	transatlantic, transcend, translate

Prefixes *continued*

Number Prefixes

Prefix	Meaning	Example
uni-	one	uniform, unit, unicycle
mono-	one	monotone, monarchy, monologue, monorail, monogram, monopoly
bi-	two	bicycle, biceps, bifocal, binocular, biplane
du-	two	duplex, duel, duplicate, duet, duo, duplicity
tri-	three	trio, triangle, triplets, trimester, tripod
qua-	four	quarter, quartet, quart, quadrangle, quadrant
pent-	five	pentagon, pentameter, pentathlon
oct-	eight	octopus, octagon, octave
cent-	hundred	centigrade, century, centimeter, centipede
semi-	half	semicircle, semiconscious, semiannual
multi-	many	multistory, multicolored, multimedia

Other Prefixes

co-, col-, con-, cor-	with, together	copilot, colleague, connect, correlate
re-	back, again	redo, regain, return, relive, rewrite, restate
auto-	self	automobile, automatic, autograph, autonomy
inter-	between, among	international, interstate, intervene, interrupt
intra-	inside	intravenous, intramural
extra-	more than usual	extrasensory, extraterrestrial, extrafine
mid-	in the middle of	midcentury, midtown, midnight, midpoint
mini-	small	miniskirt, minibike, minivan
neo-	new	neonatal, neoclassical, neolithic
socio-	relating to society	socioeconomic, sociopolitical, sociopath
under-	not enough, below	underemployed, underpowered, underweight

Greek Roots

Root	Meaning	Example
aero-	air	aerial, aerospace, aeronautics, aerosol, aeroplane (alternate spelling of airplane)
ast-	star	astronaut, astronomy, disaster, asterisk
cept-, ceive-	take	except, deceive, receive, perceive
chron-	time	chronological, synchronize, chronic, chronicle
cycl-	circle, ring	bicycle, cyclone, cycle, encyclopedia, cyclops
gram-	letter, written	telegram, diagram, grammar, epigram, monogram
graph-	write	telegraph, photograph, phonograph, autograph
meter-	measure	thermometer, centimeter, diameter, barometer
phon-	sound	phonograph, symphony, telephone, microphone, phonics
photo-	light	photograph, photography, telephoto, photosynthesis
scop-	see	microscope, telescope, periscope, stethoscope
tele-	distant	telegram, telegraph, telephone, telescope, television
therm-	heat	thermometer, thermal, thermostat, thermos

Latin Roots

Root	Meaning	Example
act-	do	action, react, transact, actor, enact
ang-	bend	angle, triangle, quadrangle, angular
aud-	hear	auditorium, audience, audiovisual, audible, audition
bio-	life	biograph, biology, biochemical, biofeedback
cred-	believe, trust	credit, discredit, incredible, credulous
dict-	speak	predict, contradict, dictate, verdict, diction
duc-, -duct-	lead	conduct, aqueduct, duct, induct, educate
fac-, fect-	make, do	factory, manufacture, facsimile, defect, perfect
fid-	faith	confident, fidelity, fiduciary, infidel
loc-	place	locate, dislocate, relocate, location, allocate
man-	hand	manufacture, manuscript, manicure, manipulate
migr-	move	migrate, immigrant, emigrate, migratory
miss-	send	missile, dismiss, missionary, mission, remiss
mob-, mot-	move	automobile, mobility, motion, motor, promote
ped-	foot	pedal, pedestrian, pedestal, pedicure
pop-	people	population, popular, populist, populace, populate
port-	carry	transport, import, export, portable, porter
rupt-	break	erupt, interrupt, rupture, bankrupt, abrupt
script-	write	script, inscription, scripture, manuscript, transcript
sect-	cut	bisect, dissect, section, intersection
sign-	mark	signature, signal, significant, insignia
spec-	see	inspect, suspect, respect, spectator, spectacle
tract-	pull, drag	tractor, subtract, attraction, traction
urb-	city	urban, suburb, suburban, urbane
vac-	empty	vacant, vacation, vacuum, evacuate, vacate
vid-	see	video, evidence, provide, providence

Suffixes

Suffix	Meaning	Example
-able, -ible	able to be	readable, legible, loveable, teachable
-al	relating to	musical, personal, mechanical, logical
-ance, -ence	state of	dependence, existence, disappearance
-er, -or, -ar, -ist	someone or something that does an action	manager, singer, director, geologist, archivist
-ful, -ous	full of	careful, doubtful, furious, jealous, courageous
-ic	nature of	poetic, heroic, platonic, harmonic
-ish	like, similar to	foolish, childish, devilish, thirtyish
-ism	belief in, practice of	idealism, Buddhism, commercialism
-ity	state or quality	sincerity, popularity, clarity
-ive	tending toward	descriptive, submissive, active
-ly	in a certain way	quickly, happily, rudely
-ment	act of, result of	enjoyment, encouragement, replacement
-ology	study of	psychology, theology, zoology
-tion, -sion	act of, process of	connection, separation, decision

Teach Basic Phonics

You have come quite a ways with your student so far. In addition to finding his or her reading levels, presenting materials on which he can succeed in reading, you are encouraging reading practice and checking comprehension. You have also helped your student develop a basic reading vocabulary with the Instant Words and basic picture nouns.

Now you can help the student further improve his or her reading by building phonics skills. Phonics is an important and useful skill associated with reading. Poor ability in phonics does not always mean poor reading ability, but if reading ability is poor, it can often be aided by making phonics lessons a part of reading instruction.

The following pages will prepare you to use the Phonics Survey and the Phonics Charts effectively.

■ The Role of Phonics

Teachers and tutors often take firm positions for or against teaching phonics. However, neither side has conclusive proof that the "phonics method" is better or worse than other methods. Since many teachers and educational researchers have found that phonics instruction (teaching the relationship between letters and sounds), *does* facilitate learning how to read and how to spell, especially for beginning readers, most teachers include some basic phonics in the reading program. It is therefore suggested that you do the same.

The charts at the end of the chapter (pages 74–82) present most of the basic phonics rules arranged in a logical teaching order.

For first-time readers in the primary grades, teachers who are advocates of phonics would start phonics instruction right away and drill the children on letter sounds and example words. They would be sure to cover the basic rules of phonics during the first grade.

A phonics moderate might start phonics lessons after the student had acquired a small sight word vocabulary (25 to 50 words). She would probably try to teach the material in the first few charts during the first year but would not be too upset with something less than perfect student performance.

A teacher who tends to drag his or her heels when it comes to phonics would take about three years to cover the material in these charts, probably skipping or at best glossing over much of the material in Chart 6 (schwa and vowel plus *r*) and Chart 7 (diphthongs and other vowel sounds).

In the course outlined above, a "year" refers to a traditional September to June year experienced by children of average ability who begin primary school at age six. Bright children, older students, and adult learners would, of course, move through these skills more quickly, but all three categories should benefit from some review lessons on phonics.

Pre-phonics

Wherever they fall along the phonics continuum, teachers and tutors would agree on the importance of first making sure that the student can make basic speech sounds of the English language and that he or she can hear the difference between these sounds. To that end, readers need to develop a skill called **phoneme awareness**. Phoneme awareness is the realization that all words are made up of relatively few sounds (phonemes) and that these same sounds come up over and over in many different words. For example, the word *cat* has three phonemes, /k/, /a/, and /t/. English uses about 44 phonemes, and these sounds are spelled (written) using hundreds of different letter combinations. Phonics is learning the correlation between the spoken sound and the letter or letter combinations that represent that sound. For example, the /k/ sound at the beginning of *cat* is spelled with the letter *c*, (not *k*), the /a/ sound with a short *a*.

You can help your students develop phoneme awareness by reading them poems that have repetition of sounds, by pointing out the same sound in similar words (see the Phonics Charts at the end of this chapter), and by discussing other word patterns such as *phonograms,* or word families (see phonogram charts on pages 83–88).

You can readily see evidence of early phonics instruction when students use invented spelling—trying to spell a word simply by how it sounds. After seeing the spelling that emerges from such attempts, you can give lessons in the appropriate phonics principle(s) to help the students spell the word more accurately. They may still resort to invented spelling from time to time, but spelling will improve with additional phonics instruction.

Periodic drills using the picture charts (pages 74–77) can also be a great help to students in hearing and making the sounds presented.

Whether or not to say the sounds in isolation is for you to decide. Some teachers who do so take care not to use a "schwa" sound (the vowel sound much like that of a short /u/, or *uh* sound) at the end of a consonant when it isn't needed. For example, in modeling the /n/ sound in the word *nice* you can say "nnn," not "nuh." Consonants that can be pronounced without a schwa sound are *t, n, r, m, s, l, p, f, v, h, k, w,* and the digraphs. (A **digraph** refers to two letters that represent a single sound, such as the *ch* in *chimney*. Consonant digraphs that usually stand for specific single sounds are *ch, sh, th,* and *wh*.)

Some teachers say that the sounds should be taught only as part of a word. Others say it is all right to pronounce a consonant with a vowel, but even teachers in this camp are divided; some would teach the sounds in the word *cat* as *c* + *at*, others as *ca* + *t*. In any case, the main goal of phonics is for the student to learn that the letter or digraph (two letters making one sound) stands for a sound. It is also very helpful to learn common letter clusters, like *-ump*, in order to read and spell other words in that "family," such as *bump, clump, dump,* and so on.

Diagnosing Phonics Skills

In phonics instruction, as in teaching any skill, a good teacher must know the student's skill level at the start of instruction, about midway through, and at the end of instruction.

As an informal test of a student's phonics ability, you can ask him or her to "sound out" unfamiliar words or syllables. You might write a single letter or a digraph such as *sh* on the board and ask the student what sound it makes. To be a bit trickier, ask the learner to sound out some nonsense syllables, taking care to build into the nonsense words the phonics skill you wish to test. For example, if you want to know if your student knows the material on Chart 4 (consonant digraphs and second sounds), write *phiz*; if he says *fizz*, you can tell that he knows some phonics.

The Phonics Survey on page 73 will help you to assess a student's skills systematically in the main phonics areas.

Methods of Teaching Phonics

Phonics Charts. The Phonics Charts at the end of this chapter give you a fairly complete overview of the phonics usually taught in most schools. Page through these charts to get a general idea. They are arranged in a teaching order, with the suggestion that you first teach the content of Chart 1, then Chart 2, and so on.

Phonics is simply a method of teaching the letter-sound connection, so don't worry if your student can't read all the words on the charts. The picture in each box of words in Charts 1–4, for example, is just a visual cue to help the student recognize the sound that the featured letter makes. (Saying the word *ring*, pictured in Chart 1, models the /r/ sound of words in that box.)

As mentioned earlier, sometimes two letters make one sound. You should teach these two-letter combinations, called digraphs, as if they were a single letter. For example, the digraph *sh* combines the sound of /s/ and /h/ but forms a new sound (phoneme) different from either letter. The main consonant digraphs are *ch, sh, th,* and *wh*; the digraph *th* can be voiced, as in *this*, or voiceless, as in *thin*.

In a **blend,** two different consonant sounds occur together so that both are sounded, for example, as the *bl* in *black*. It is different from a consonant digraph like *sh*, which makes one sound only.

You will also note that all vowels and certain consonants (for example, the letters *c* and *g*) have several sounds, a concept that can be confusing for a student. The letter *c* has a /k/ sound when it comes before *a, o,* and *u;* but it generally has an /s/ sound before *i, e,* and *y*. The letter *g* can have the sound of hard /g/ or of /j/. And the letter *s* can have an /s/ or a /z/ sound. Practicing and gradually mastering the skills on these charts in the order presented will cut down on the confusion.

Encourage your student to apply phonics when he is reading and can't pronounce a particular word. You can say, "Try sounding it out" and then help the student do it. If sounding out a whole word is too difficult, you can just ask the student what sound the word begins with. Or you can say, "What other words do you know that have parts that look like parts of this word?"

When trying to sound out unfamiliar words, however, you will quickly find that phonics rules don't always help. There are more phonics rules than those presented on the charts that follow, and there are many exceptions to the rules. Why should the word *sugar*, for example, have a *sh* sound at the beginning, or why does *of* have an *uv* sound? There aren't enough rules to account for all the exceptions, which is why *many words have to be learned as sight words*. But don't despair; phonics does help in unlocking many words and parts of words that have regular spellings. For this reason, the rules are useful in some spelling lessons. Phonics rules also often help the student sound out just part of an unfamiliar word. For example, the first thing many reading teachers say when a student is stuck on a word is, "What sound does it begin with?" With that information plus help from the context, the student can often pronounce the word.

Nobody said that learning to read (or improving reading skills) was easy. It takes practice over a period of time, the length of which will depend on the learner. She or he needs all the reading help available, using any method that works. Phonics is just one method to aid the reading process.

You can use the Phonics Charts to introduce basic principles such as easy consonants or short vowels. Reinforce your instruction by giving students enough practice with these sounds by using practice words and games, and by calling attention to these sounds when reading.

Games.   Just as it does for teaching Instant Words, **Bingo** works well for teaching phonics. Make some bingo cards of the sounds on Chart 1 (page 74) and call off the letter sounds, one at a time. When calling letters, remember to use a letter sound (say "*ss* as in Sam"), *not* a letter name such as "dee" for the *d* sound, "es" for the *s* sound, and so on. Remember to use the same letters on each bingo card but with a different arrangement on each card.

You can also make card decks for different versions of the **Pairs** game, printing consonant sounds on the cards instead of Instant Words, as discussed in Step 4.

T	N	R
M	D	S
L	C	P

Bingo Card for Beginners

B	F	V	A	H
K	W	J	QU	X
Y	Z	TH	CH	WH
SH	PH	PR	ST	PL
TW	GL	SN	FR	SK

Bingo Card for More Advanced Students

Spelling. Some teachers are quite successful teaching phonics along with spelling and writing. After an initial presentation of the first half of Phonics Charts 1 and 2 (easy consonants and easy vowels), a teacher might have a group of students write a word, for example *sad,* on a sheet of paper. After a minute, a volunteer from the group writes the word correctly on the board. This exercise provides each student with immediate feedback of results, an effective learning aid. Of course, the teacher should choose only phonetically regular words from among the sounds already introduced.

Some teachers even call off nonsense words, such as *dat* and *nuv,* for students to spell just to test their phonics skills. Others are more concerned that students know the meaning of each word they write. To that end these teachers often ask students to use each word in a sentence.

Keep in mind that students sometimes need to know how to spell a word right away, for example, when writing notes or letters they must send at once without worrying about misspelled words. This is the right time to respect a student's request for instant help and give him or her the correct spelling. Other times students may be unsure of how to spell a word needed for short paragraphs or stories they are writing. To keep the focus on writing, rather than on mechanics that might trip them up, encourage students to write the word as they think it should be spelled or just write down a couple of letters of the word and some space (as a placeholder) and move on. They can go back to the word later and find its spelling or decide to use another word that means the same thing.

The *Spelling Book,* published by Teacher Created Materials, contains many suggestions for teaching phonics and shows that phonics can be taught easily and effectively in spelling lessons. As a teacher or tutor, you can decide whether to teach phonics as part of reading lessons, as part of spelling lessons, or both—which might be even better.

Phonograms. A **phonogram** is a group of letters containing a vowel and a consonant sound that needs another consonant sound to make a word. For example, the *-ail* phonogram can make **word families** like *mail, tail,* and *sail* when different initial consonants are substituted.

Phonogram is terminology used by reading teachers. Some language specialists call the same idea *onset and rhyme,* the onset being the initial consonant sound like /d/ and the rhyme the ending vowel and consonant like *-og.* Together they make the word *dog*, which rhymes with *log, fog, hog,* and so on. Other linguists call this idea *consonant substitution*.

One way to use a phonogram is simply to write it on the board or on a sheet of paper and ask your student to make as many words as possible using that phonogram. You can provide help if needed.

Lists of phonograms are also good for spelling lessons. Give several words from one or two phonogram families to your student and go over them together to make sure he can pronounce all of the words. Then give a spelling test to see if he can spell them all. This is a great way to teach the sounds of different consonants and in turn, the phonograms.

Here is another way to incorporate phonograms with spelling when students are unsure of how to spell a word. Suggest that they think of another word in the same pattern, or phonogram family, that rhymes with that word. If *sting* is the troublesome word, they might come up with *sing*. If they know the beginning letters, *s* and *t*, and also know that *sing* ends in *-ing*, they might arrive at the correct spelling.

Phonograms also can be taught in the context of several games and by using teaching devices. Word wheels, slip charts, and board games often use phonograms. You can buy these devices in school supply stores or make them yourself. A **word wheel** has a rhyme printed on a small wheel with onsets printed around the edge of the larger wheel behind it. New words are formed by turning the larger wheel. This device provides the repetitive practice necessary for learning. A **slip chart** is similar to a word wheel in concept. A rhyme is printed on a card with a slot cut out on the left side. Onsets are printed on a strip narrower than the card slot. To make a word, slide the strip through the opening of the rhyme card, as you would a buckle.

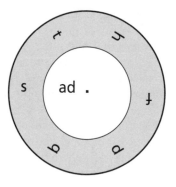

Word Wheel

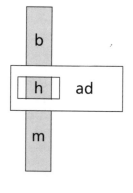

Slip Chart

At the end of this chapter (pages 83–88) you will find several phonogram families and example words to use for teaching. There are many more phonograms, but these will get you started. You can find long lists of phonograms (and other useful word lists for teaching) in *The Reading Teacher's Book of Lists* published by Prentice Hall.

A Word of Caution

The benefit of teaching phonics is that it helps students sound out unfamiliar words and make rapid progress in reading. The downside is that some teachers "beat it to death" with boring drills, and the student learns to hate reading and education in general.

Another caution about phonics is that of placing too much emphasis on sounds and not enough on other important reading skills such as comprehension. Over-emphasis on sounds can turn students into wordcallers, spitting out words orally with no idea of their meaning.

Keep the "phun" in phonics by using the method to its best advantage—as one of several components of a balanced reading program. Let your lessons incorporate word review, oral reading, phonics, silent reading, comprehension exercises and discussion, spelling lessons, writing, and plenty of easy reading practice with relevant material that holds student interest.

STEP 5 RESOURCES

Phonics Survey Directions

The survey on the following page will give you a general idea of your student's level of phonics development. Such information will be quite useful in selecting materials for phonics instruction. You can retest your student at a later date after giving additional phonics instruction. In the meantime you can make up more nonsense words for testing or teaching.

Directions:

How to Test. Ask the student to read the nonsense words aloud, letting him or her know that they are not real words. If the student makes an error, allow a second chance but not a third.

How to Score. Using a copy of the survey, circle each letter read incorrectly. In the boxes to the right of the words in each section, check the student's responses as *Perfect, Knew Some,* or *Knew None* for the following skills: consonants, short vowels, long vowels, and difficult vowels.

Phonics Survey

Name _____

Date _____

	Perfect	Knew Some	Knew None

Section 1: Easy Consonants and Short Vowels
(Charts 1 and 2)

			Perfect	Knew Some	Knew None
TIF	NEL	ROM	☐	☐	☐
DUP	CAV	SEB	☐	☐	☐

Section 2: Harder Consonants and Long Vowels
(Charts 3 and 5)

					Perfect	Knew Some	Knew None
KO	HOAB	WAJE	KE	YATE	☐	☐	☐
ZEEX	QUIDE	YAIG	ZAY	SUDE	☐	☐	☐

Section 3: Consonant Digraphs and Difficult Vowels
(Charts 4, 6, and 7)

				Perfect	Knew Some	Knew None
WHAW	THOIM	PHER	KOYCH	☐	☐	☐
OUSH	CHAU	EANG	HOON	☐	☐	☐

Phonics Charts

Phonics Chart 1: Easy Consonants

T — table
to
take
tell
not
at
it

N — nut
not
no
new
and
in
can

R — ring
run
red
read
from
our
for

M — man
me
mother
some
from
room
lemon

D — dog
do
day
down
good
and
said

S — saw
some
so
see
this
us
yes

L — letter
little
like
look
will
wall
school

C — cat
can
come
color
because
second
music

P — pencil
put
pretty
page
up
jump
stop

B — book
but
be
boy
about
remember
tub

F — fish
for
from
first
if
before
off

V — valentine
very
visit
voice
give
leave
have

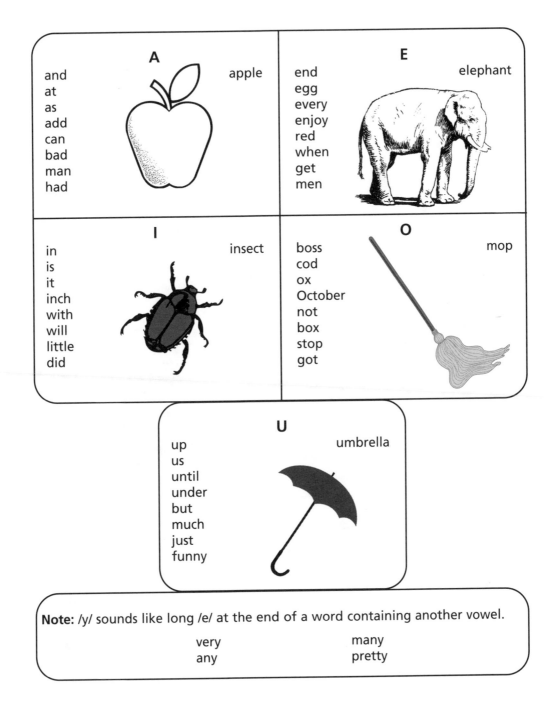

A   apple

and
at
as
add
can
bad
man
had

E   elephant

end
egg
every
enjoy
red
when
get
men

I   insect

in
is
it
inch
with
will
little
did

O   mop

boss
cod
ox
October
not
box
stop
got

U   umbrella

up
us
until
under
but
much
just
funny

Note: /y/ sounds like long /e/ at the end of a word containing another vowel.

very   many
any   pretty

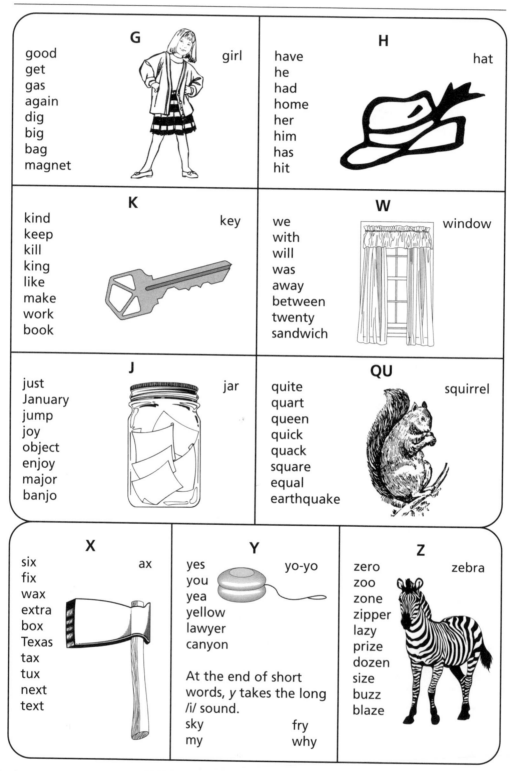

G

good
get
gas
again
dig
big
bag
magnet

girl

H

have
he
had
home
her
him
has
hit

hat

K

kind
keep
kill
king
like
make
work
book

key

W

we
with
will
was
away
between
twenty
sandwich

window

J

just
January
jump
joy
object
enjoy
major
banjo

jar

QU

quite
quart
queen
quick
quack
square
equal
earthquake

squirrel

X

six
fix
wax
extra
box
Texas
tax
tux
next
text

ax

Y

yes
you
yea
yellow
lawyer
canyon

yo-yo

At the end of short
words, y takes the long
/i/ sound.
sky   fry
my   why

Z

zero
zoo
zone
zipper
lazy
prize
dozen
size
buzz
blaze

zebra

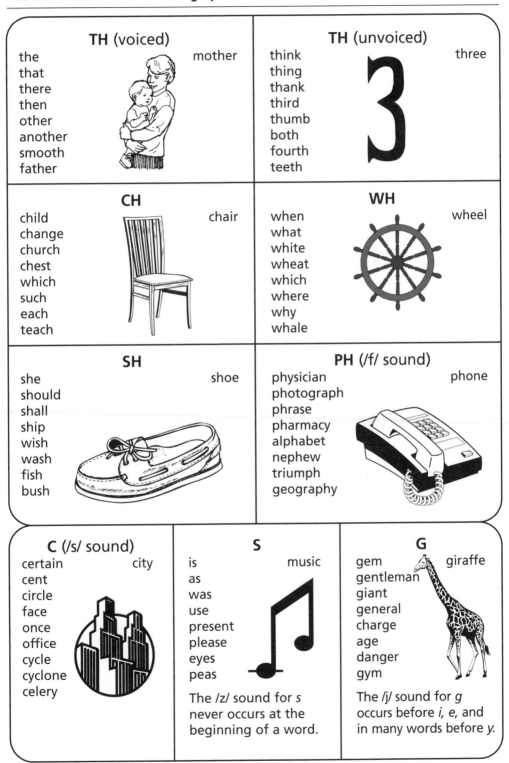

TH (voiced)

the
that
there
then
other
another
smooth
father

mother

TH (unvoiced)

think
thing
thank
third
thumb
both
fourth
teeth

three

CH

child
change
church
chest
which
such
each
teach

chair

WH

when
what
white
wheat
which
where
why
whale

wheel

SH

she
should
shall
ship
wish
wash
fish
bush

shoe

PH (/f/ sound)

physician
photograph
phrase
pharmacy
alphabet
nephew
triumph
geography

phone

C (/s/ sound)

certain
cent
circle
face
once
office
cycle
cyclone
celery

city

S

is
as
was
use
present
please
eyes
peas

music

The /z/ sound for *s* never occurs at the beginning of a word.

G

gem
gentleman
giant
general
charge
age
danger
gym

giraffe

The /j/ sound for *g* occurs before *i, e,* and in many words before *y.*

Final *e* Rule: An *e* at the end of a word frequently makes the preceding vowel long and the *e* silent.

A-E		**O-E**	
make	ate	robe	bone
sale	age	code	hope
came	ace	joke	nose
made	able	hole	note
plane	ape	home	stove
I-E		**U-E**	
rice	time	tube	fume
wife	fire	dude	tune
five	nine	true	blue
write	mile	nuke	use
ride	like	mule	cute

Note: The long /e/ sound before final *e* (such as in the word *theme*) is omitted because of its relative infrequency.

Exception to final *e* rule: In a few words, final *e* does **not** indicate that the preceding vowel is long.

are	come
one	some

Open Syllable Rule: When a syllable ends in a vowel, that vowel frequently has the long sound.

A	E	I	O	U
April	we	I	so	duty
paper	be	idea	ago	pupil
later	helix	pilot	no	music
baby	meter	tiny	open	student
radio	even	lion	hello	January

Double Vowel Rule: When two vowels are together, frequently the first vowel is long and the second one is silent. These are also known as vowel digraphs. There are only six common ones.

AI	AY	EA	EE	OA	OW
aid	day	eat	see	oak	own
fail	pay	year	feet	coat	grown
remain	stay	please	seem	soap	show
train	clay	easy	sleep	road	yellow
wait	crayon	sea	tree	loan	bowl

Schwa: The unaccented vowel in a word having two or more syllables frequently has the sound of the *a* in *ago*, much like a short /u/ sound.

/ə/ **A**	/ə/ **E**	/ə/ **O**
about	happen	atom
again	problem	riot
comma	bulletin	oppose
several	taken	money
China	united	canyon

/ur/ sound: *er, ir,* and *ur* frequently all make the same /ur/ sound.

ER	**IR**	**UR**
her	sir	fur
were	first	turn
other	dirt	hurt
germ	third	hurry
camera	circus	Thursday

ar **has two sounds:**
(1) broad /a/ sound, as in *far*;
(2) short /e/ sound, as in *vary*.   *or* **has a unique /o/ sound,** as in *for*.

AR		**OR**	
broad /a/ /är/	short /e/ /ĕ/		
far	vary	for	fork
start	library	or	cord
are	Mary	before	storm
dark	care	more	short
hard	January	porch	
carp	share		

Phonics Chart 7: Diphthongs and Other Vowel Sounds

Broad /o/ sound is made mainly by *o, al, aw,* and *au.*

O /ô/	**AL** /ô/	**AW** /ô/	**AU** /ô/
boss	all	draw	because
long	salt	craw	auto
cost	also	awful	August
off	talk	lawn	haul
cloth	call	straw	daughter

Diphthongs make a sliding sound from one vowel to another.

OI **OY**	**OU** **OW**
oi and *oy* make the same /oi/ sound.	*ou* and *ow* make the same /ou/ sound.
oil boy	out how
point annoy	about down
voice enjoy	our brown
noise royal	round owl
coin oyster	loud flower

Double /o/ and the second sound of *ea*

OO		**EA** (second sound)
/o͞o/	/o͝o/	short /e/ sound: /ĕ/
(long sound)	(short sound)	dead weather
soon	good	ahead health
school	foot	heavy heaven
too	look	ready bread
room	cook	feather thread
truth	put	

Silent letters

KN *k* before *n* is silent.	**GH** *gh* is usually silent.
knife knot	eight light
knee knight	high caught
know knit	might taught

r Family

BR	CR	DR	FR	GR	PR	TR
bread	crab	dress	free	grand	pretty	trick
brick	cry	drug	frog	grapes	prince	truck
bring	crow	drum	from	green	prize	true
zebra	across	hundred	afraid	hungry	April	extra

l Family

BL	CL	FL	GL	PL	SL
black	class	flag	glad	plate	slap
blue	clock	flower	glass	play	slow
blood	cloud	fly	glory	please	sled
tumbler	include	snowflake	igloo	supply	asleep

s Family

SC	SK	SM	SN	SP	ST	SW
scan	skate	smart	snap	space	stamp	sweep
scout	sky	smell	snow	spoon	stop	swell
scoop	skin	smile	snake	sport	stone	swim
disc	mask	smoke	snooze	crisp	best	swing

s Family

SCR	STR	SPR
scrape	strap	spray
scream	strike	spread
screw	strip	spring
scrub	strong	sprinkle

Orphans

TW	DW
twelve	dwarf
twice	dweeb
twins	dwell
between	dwindle

Phonograms

-ack /ă/	-ad /ă/	-an /ă/	-ash /ă/
back	bad	an	ash
hack	cad	ban	bash
jack	dad	can	cash
lack	fad	Dan	dash
pack	had	fan	gash
rack	lad	man	hash
sack	mad	pan	lash
tack	pad	ran	mash
black	sad	tan	rash
crack	Brad	van	sash
slack	Chad	bran	clash
track	clad	clan	crash
shack	glad	flan	flash
whack	shad	plan	slash
smack		scan	smash
snack		span	stash
stack		than	trash
			thrash

-at /ă/	-ail /ā/	-ain /ā/	-ake /ā/
at	ail	gain	bake
bat	bail	lain	cake
cat	fail	main	fake
fat	Gail	pain	Jake
hat	hail	rain	lake
mat	jail	vain	make
pat	mail	brain	rake
rat	nail	chain	sake
sat	pail	drain	take
tat	rail	grain	wake
vat	sail	plain	brake
brat	tail	slain	drake
chat	wail	Spain	flake
flat	frail	sprain	quake
slat	quail	stain	shake
scat	snail	strain	snake
spat	trail	train	
that			

-ate /ā/	-ay /ā/	-ar /ä/	-ead /ĕ/
ate	bay	bar	dead
date	day	car	head
fate	gay	far	lead
gate	hay	jar	read
hate	jay	tar	bread
Kate	lay	char	dread
late	may	star	tread
mate	nay		spread
rate	pay	**-ard /ä/**	thread
crate	ray	card	
grate	say	guard	**-eck /ĕ/**
plate	way	hard	deck
skate	clay	lard	heck
slate	play	yard	neck
state	gray		peck
	tray	**art /ä/**	check
	stay	cart	speck
		part	wreck
		chart	
		smart	
		start	

-ed /ĕ/	-ell /ĕ/	-ent /ĕ/	-ea /ē/
bed	bell	bent	pea
fed	cell	cent	sea
led	dell	dent	tea
Ned	fell	lent	flea
red	hell	rent	plea
Ted	jell	sent	
wed	Nell	tent	**-eat /ē/**
bled	sell	went	eat
fled	tell	spent	beat
sled	well		feat
bred	yell	**-est /ĕ/**	heat
Fred	quell	best	meat
shed	shell	nest	neat
sped	smell	pest	peat
shred	spell	rest	seat
	dwell	test	cheat
	swell	vest	bleat
		west	cleat
		chest	pleat
		crest	treat
			wheat

-eed /ē/
deed
feed
heed
need
reed
seed
weed
bleed
breed
creed
freed
greed
speed
steed
tweed

-eep /ē/
beep
deep
jeep
keep
peep
seep
weep
creep
sheep
sleep
steep
sweep

-ief /ē/
brief
chief
grief
thief

-ield /ē/
field
yield
shield

-ick /ĭ/
kick
lick
nick
pick
Rick
sick
tick
wick
brick
trick
chick
thick
click
flick
slick
quick
stick

-id /ĭ/
bid
did
hid
kid
lid
rid
grid
skid
slid

-ig /ĭ/
big
dig
fig
gig
jig
pig
rig
wig
brig
sprig
twig

-ing /ĭ/
ding
king
ping
ring
sing
wing
bring
fling
sling
sting
spring
string
swing
thing

-ish /ĭ/
dish
fish
wish
swish

-ight /ī/
fight
light
might
night
right
sight
tight
bright
fright
flight
plight
slight

-ime /ī/
dime
lime
time
chime
crime
grime
slime

-ice /ī/
ice
dice
lice
mice
nice
rice
vice
price
slice
twice

-ide /ī/
bide
hide
ride
side
tide
wide
bride
glide
slide

-ipe /ī/
pipe
ripe
wipe
gripe
swipe

-y /ī/
by
my
cry
dry
fly
fry
shy
sky
try
why

-ond /ŏ/
bond
fond
pond
blond

-op /ŏ/
cop
hop
mop
pop
top
chop
crop
drop
prop
flop
plop
shop
slop
stop

-ot /ŏ/
cot
dot
got
hot
jot
lot
not
pot
rot
blot
clot
plot
slot
shot
spot
trot

-ox /ŏ/
ox
box
fox
lox
pox

-o /ō/
go
no
so
pro

-oach /ō/
coach
poach
roach
broach

-oke /ō/
coke
joke
poke
woke
yoke
choke
broke
smoke
spoke
stroke

-old /ō/
old
bold
fold
gold
hold
mold
sold
told
scold

-ope /ō/
cope
dope
hope
mope
rope
scope
slope

-ose /ō/
hose
nose
pose
rose
chose
those
close

-ow /ō/
bow
low
mow
row
sow
tow
blow
flow
glow
slow
crow
grow
show

-ood /o͞o/
good
hood
wood
stood

-ook /o͞o/
book
cook
hook
look
took
crook
shook

-ould /o͞o/
could
would
should

-ew /o͞o/
dew
new
pew
blew
flew
stew
brew
crew
drew
grew
chew
screw

-oo /o͞o/
boo
coo
goo
moo
too
woo
zoo

-oom /o͞o/
boom
doom
room
zoom
bloom
broom
gloom
groom

-oose /o͞o/
goose
loose
moose
noose

-oup /o͞o/
soup
croup
group

-all /ô/
ball
call
fall
gall
hall
mall
pall
tall
wall
small
stall

-alk /ô/
balk
talk
walk
chalk
stalk

-alt /ô/
halt
malt
salt

-aught /ô/
caught
naught
taught

-aunch /ô/
haunch
launch
paunch
staunch

-ause /ô/
cause
pause
clause

aw /ô/
caw
jaw
law
paw
raw
saw
claw
flaw
draw
straw

-awn /ô/
dawn
fawn
lawn
pawn
yawn
drawn

-ong /ô/
gong
long
song
tong
prong
thong
wrong
strong

-oss /ô/
boss
loss
moss
toss
cross
floss

-ost /ô/
cost
lost
frost

-ore /or/
bore
core
fore
gore
more
pore
sore
tore
wore
chore
shore
score
spore
store
swore

-ork /or/
cork
fork
pork
stork

-oil /oi/
boil
coil
foil
soil
toil
broil
spoil

-oin /oi/
coin
join
loin
groin

-oint /oi/
joint
point

-oy /oi/
boy
coy
joy
soy
toy
ploy

-ound /ou/
bound
found
hound
mound
pound
round
sound
wound
ground

-oud /ou/
loud
cloud
proud

-our /ou/
our
sour
flour
scour

-ouse /ou/
house
louse
mouse
blouse

-out /ou/
bout
gout
pout
clout
scout
shout
snout
spout
trout
sprout

-outh /ou/
mouth
south

-ow /ou/	**-ub /ŭ/**	**-uck /ŭ/**	**-uff /ŭ/**
bow	cub	buck	buff
cow	dub	duck	cuff
how	hub	luck	huff
now	nub	muck	muff
vow	pub	puck	puff
wow	rub	suck	bluff
chow	sub	tuck	gruff
brow	tub	chuck	stuff
plow	club	shuck	
	flub	cluck	**-ug /ŭ/**
-own /ou/	grub	pluck	bug
down	snub	stuck	dug
gown	stub	truck	hug
town	scrub	struck	jug
brown	shrub		lug
clown		**-ud /ŭ/**	mug
crown		bud	rug
drown		mud	tug
frown		crud	drug
		spud	plug
		stud	smug
		thud	snug

-ump /ŭ/	**-un /ŭ/**	**-erk /ur/**	**-irt /ur/**
bump	bun	jerk	dirt
dump	fun	perk	flirt
hump	gun	clerk	shirt
jump	nun		skirt
lump	pun	**-erm /ur/**	
pump	run	germ	**-ur /ur/**
rump	sun	term	cur
sump	shun	sperm	fur
chump	spun		blur
clump	stun	**-ir /ur/**	slur
frump		fir	
grump	**-ust /ŭ/**	sir	**-urse /ur/**
plump	bust	stir	curse
slump	dust		nurse
stump	just	**-irl /ur/**	purse
	lust	girl	
	must	swirl	**-urt /ur/**
	rust	twirl	curt
	crust	whirl	hurt
	trust		blurt
	thrust		spurt

Build Writing, Speaking, and Listening Skills

The overview of this book regarding Step 6 discusses the idea of building and improving writing, speaking, and listening skills by integrating them into reading lessons instead of addressing them all as separate lessons, as in the past. It is an important concept but not a new or even a particularly sophisticated one, as the following example illustrates.

Other cultures have long accomplished the job of teaching reading and language skills through a practice that today might be described as a "minimalist" kind of school—simple yet maintaining a structure or framework. One such school consisted of a tree, a chair, and a small box of books. There was no furniture for the students; they sat on bare ground. This school had no walls, no windows, no electricity, no chalkboard, no basal-style readers, practically no library, and no pencils or paper.

Yet this "no frills" school had certain advantages. The setting was beautiful: birds sang and butterflies floated through the "classroom." The air was fresh and the lighting excellent. No bells rang to start or end lessons and no administration set down rules. The teacher had to be creative, and he was. He was conducting a very effective elementary reading lesson. You might wonder how, when he had nothing—perhaps not quite nothing. He *did* have knowledge of some basic teaching techniques, and he had a long, straight stick.

Before you think the worst about the purpose for the stick, let's just call it a basic school supply. The teacher used it to smooth a section of bare ground. Then, with a twig plucked from a nearby bush, he had the students draw lines in the dirt, using the stick as a ruler. On those lines students wrote stories in small groups, with one student writing, others helping with suggestions for a topic and with spelling, and then all students reading the story when it was written. The students worked in groups, and one group read the other's stories and talked about them. The teacher helped the students get started, aided in correcting spelling and grammar, and took full advantage of the relaxed atmosphere to promote creative writing while he acted as facilitator to get the story written and read. Later he had most of the students write words from the story in the smoothed dirt using twigs.

The students were proud to show off their stories, reading and talking about them, then listening to those of the other students. In light of this true experience, it is hard not to take with a grain of salt the familiar complaints of a teacher who says he can't teach reading well without the proper books, enough books or supplies, a new chalkboard, or a well-equipped classroom.

■ Language Experience Approach

The method the teacher was using is well known in the United States and is called various names, such as the language experience approach, or the whole language method. It focuses on creating meaning and has been successful in helping students learn to read and in helping poor readers improve their reading and writing skills. The language experience/whole language approach is so named because it integrates reading, writing, speaking, and listening—the basic components of language. The more someone knows about a particular topic, the more meaningful it is to him or her. What a person knows and thinks about he or she can talk about, and what one talks about can be expressed in writing. The language experience approach, therefore, draws upon the student's prior knowledge and life experiences as a basis for reading instruction. It involves three basic ideas.

1. Motivate the student (or a group) to write a story.
2. Have most of students read the story.
3. Discuss it, extend it, correct it, and read it again.

Sounds simple, doesn't it? You'd think that teachers and tutors would use this technique all the time, but there are some reasons they don't. Many teachers find it difficult to get students' creative juices flowing often enough. In addition, many teachers rely on books to extend the student's reading and critical thinking experiences instead of the students themselves as the source of the learning experience. Finally, not everyone learns in the same way. Some students do best with a more structured approach, which might include basic sight vocabularies, phonics, and a variety of comprehension questions.

These reasons notwithstanding, language experience can show the link between thought and oral language as written language produced through dictation. A great many teachers successfully incorporate story writing and some whole language teaching into traditional reading lessons. And so can you—that is, once you have chosen a topic.

Story Starters

Getting an individual or a group of students to write a story is sometimes likened to pulling teeth, so the wise teacher or tutor often has a few techniques to help the writing get started. Some teachers get students to talk about a recent or relevant personal experience they have had, such as what they did on a trip, a new procedure at work, a job change, the birth of a child, or a popular news event.

Another way to get the ball rolling is to have students use a story starter, which is a phrase or suggested title such as

My favorite place to be . . .

Don't you hate it when . . .

In the year 2020 . . .

There are additional story starters at the end of this chapter. After considering them, you and your students might end up altering an existing one from the list or, with a little brainstorming, settle on a new one tailored to their interests and background. (As suggested in Step 2, some of the items on the student Interest Inventory also make good story starters.)

Using the Language Experience Approach

An aspect of the language experience approach to story writing often used with beginning readers, who have very limited writing ability, is that of the student-made **experience chart.** Basically, the students dictate a short story or personal experience while the teacher or tutor writes it down on a large piece of paper, a chalkboard, or keys it into a computer. After the teacher reads the story to verify its message with the students, they read the story to the teacher. You can use this approach with a single student or a small group.

Choose a Topic. To get started, you can invite the student (or group) to brainstorm and gather ideas on a topic of interest and perhaps a title. Or you can take the initiative, if necessary, and suggest a story starter as a topic or even show a picture from a magazine or a book and ask them what is happening.

After a title is written down, you can help the dictation by saying something like, *Now what do you want to say about . . . ?*

Record the Students' Words. The teacher must be careful to write (print) the students' words using short, easy sentences. It is all right for the teacher to modify the dictation a bit by keeping the vocabulary easy and by writing words conventionally that are simply mispronounced or spoken with a heavy dialect. Especially for beginning readers, the story should be very short. Remember that the student or students are going to have to read back the whole story and learn to read all the new words used.

Note that the experience chart need not be completed in one lesson. You might write just a sentence or two, then add to the story at the next session. Of course, at each lesson you should review the parts of the story written earlier. Have the student(s) try to read it, with as little help from the teacher as possible.

Read the Story. The instructor reads the story back to the students to verify what they wrote and to check whether they want to make changes to it. You can ask your students to read the story with you, sentence by sentence. Shy students might feel encouraged if you remind them that they already know what the sentence says because the words are their own.

Select Words from the Story. With input from the students, you should take selected words out of the story and see if they can still read them out of context, that is, separate from the stories. This technique prevents students from merely memorizing the whole story and not really knowing how to read the individual words. It is not *bad* for the student to become so familiar with a story that it is almost memorized, but make sure that the student also knows how to read all the words in the story for a more productive reading lesson. You might wish to review the other techniques in Step 4 for teaching individual words.

Reread the Story. Suggest that the students read the story in chorus with you. Reading in phrases and sentences, and reading more than one sentence at a time will help them better think of the story as a whole. When the students seem comfortable with the story, have them read it on their own. Rereading also gives them a chance to read for meaning and increases reading fluency.

You should also check student comprehension of the story just so they get the idea that, for all kinds of reading, comprehension is essential. Step 3 has several suggestions on varying the types of questions you ask, along with other techniques for teaching comprehension.

Give Students the Story. Writing the student stories on a sheet of paper or on a large paper chart has one advantage over a chalkboard: they can be saved and read later, at the end of a week, a month, or even a year. Sometimes students like to look back at earlier lessons to see how far they have come in reading more advanced material. You can also give them cards with key words from the story, especially ones they need to practice. They will progress from simple story dictation to writing stories, but at this early level it is important that students see their own spoken words in written form.

As advised for all kinds of reading and writing lessons discussed so far, keep the experience charts easy enough for your student to be successful with them. Frustrate him or her too often and you won't *have* a student—there may be a body present, but the mind will be elsewhere.

■ Other Writing

Student-Written Stories

As students develop skill in writing, they can write their own stories. Most educators now urge student writers to use invented spelling on their first draft. This means that the student should write the story to get the ideas down and worry about correct spelling later. The same is true for grammar, which can be corrected on a later draft.

Not every story has to be polished. Sometimes the student can just write a short, interesting story or paragraph and read it to the teacher or to the group. Other times the student should take the time to polish a story by having the teacher or another in the group look it over and suggest improved spelling or grammar.

Incidentally, writing is developmental in the same way that reading and speaking are. In speaking, for example, a child first babbles, then speaks in one word sentences, then with simple vocabulary and slightly longer sentences. At first, speech sounds are not complete, and some words come out mispronounced in "baby talk." The process is the same in writing, but it happens at an older age. Writing development begins with scribbling, progresses to crude letters, then to invented spelling, then to short stories with simple vocabulary, and later to more mature writing. So don't be concerned if beginning writers are not perfect writers. Help them to progress in small steps. Give plenty of encouragement at every stage, and don't criticize mistakes but instead call attention to them gently, if at all. Not every story needs to be a showpiece; getting the ideas down is more important. Lastly, build in enough practice time for students to gain fluency in writing.

Older students and adults might enjoy writing entire short books of their collected stories or personal experiences. Some teachers type these student stories and bind them, including student art as illustrations. If you have several students, they might enjoy reading and commenting on each other's stories and books.

Reading Numbers

Because many of your students are not first-time readers, they may already know how to read numbers. Some developing readers, though, often have trouble reading numbers, particularly large numbers. Review reading numbers with your students to see which kinds are troublesome. You can start out teaching low numbers like 22, 96, 45 and work your way up to large ones, such as 123, 541, or 8,700.

Expository Writing

Discussion in this step thus far has dealt with writing as though stories are the only things students read, but this is not so. Expository writing simply refers to any kind of nonfiction material that is not a story, such as autobiographies, newspaper stories, textbook material, a set of directions, letters, and advertisements. Your student will need to practice writing and reading this type of material also.

One technique to try with students who have some reading and vocabulary skills but feel intimidated at the thought of writing an entire passage is that of the **story framework.** In such a framework (a variation on the cloze procedure), the structure of the passage is already built in and the student fills in the blanks with his or her own words and ideas. Later the student may want to copy the entire passage in manuscript or cursive writing or type it on a computer. Below is an example of a story framework.

My Autobiography

My name is _____. I was born in the state of _____.
I spent most of my childhood in _____. The memories
of growing up are _____ memories. There were _____ children in
my family. The best part of growing up was _____
_____.

Now I am older and I live in _____. I am _____
_____ and I have _____ children. The best part of my life now
is _____.

Adult developing readers and writers appreciate the functional benefit of learning expository writing and reading. In many adult classes, the writing gets very practical. Students fill out job applications, insurance and medical forms, and write work reports or notes to school for their children.

Keep in mind that learning to write helps learning to read, and learning to read helps learning to write. So encourage practice in both.

Handwriting

There are several popular methods of forming letters. At the end of this chapter are two charts, one of a **manuscript alphabet** (printing) and the other of a **cursive alphabet** (handwriting), representing one method that is widely used. Most schools and adult learning centers will give out a copy of the handwriting chart they use.

Manuscript. Teachers usually begin with manuscript writing because it seems easier for new writers. And since most forms and applications require that the person completing them do so by printing, learning manuscript writing gives learners a practical skill that is immediately applicable. Even though older students and adults have *seen* printed words for most of their lives, actually forming the letters on paper is a different experience. Have them practice on just a few letters at a time and then combine the letters into words. All beginners, regardless of age, need occasional correction and sometimes additional practice on letters that they form poorly.

Cursive. After your students have learned manuscript writing, you can teach them the cursive alphabet. For some, learning cursive writing is important so that they can write the way other adults write. This can be especially true for school, community, or other group meetings where there is often a sign-in sheet that everyone will see.

If students show an interest in learning cursive, it is worth the time it takes to make it legible. Document examiners say that a well-written name is much more difficult to forge than a sloppy one. A bank employee who sees a sloppy signature on a check or other document might wonder whether it was forged. Having said that, however, instead of spending too much time on handwriting specifically, you might incorporate its practice into other aspects of your reading program. For example, students can practice handwriting while they write out spelling words.

Note that it is not at all uncommon for students to make faster progress in reading than in writing, so don't hold back your students in reading just because they cannot write (or spell) all the words in that lesson. Just keep moving ahead in reading but give the student continued practice in writing skills.

Just Manuscript? Most people use cursive for everyday writing. Although this is the popular custom, it is not absolutely necessary to learn cursive writing, so don't be concerned if your student shows little or no interest in learning it. (In Europe many people use manuscript handwriting their whole lives.) Some educators argue that only manuscript handwriting (printing) should be taught because it is more legible than cursive and can be written just as quickly. Incidentally, manuscript is legal as signatures on checks and other legal documents so long as that is what the person consistently uses as a signature.

Another argument for teaching only manuscript is that it helps students see the printed words and match the style of print they encounter in books and newspapers, so that reading and writing begin to reinforce each other. In addition, since manuscript resembles the look of typewritten material, it serves as a kind of bridge to learning how to type.

Typing. Developing readers and writers often regard the look of their typewritten assignments as more "adult," or professional. Another, more practical, reason to learn typing, or keyboarding, is that more and more jobs today require keyboarding skills. In addition, in some high schools and colleges, themes and papers must be typed, so students very often use computers for homework assignments.

When students reach the third or fourth grade ability, they can start learning to type. Using the traditional 10-finger "touch" system is advised before they fall into the "hunt and peck" method, a habit difficult to break. Touch typing is not hard to learn; it takes only about four weeks of lessons. If your students wish to try it, suggest that they practice on a typewriter or on a personal computer with a word processing program. They can follow the lessons in *Computer Keyboarding for Beginners* (Edward Fry, Ph.D.), a compact manual published by Teacher Created Materials. A little discipline and practice should reward students with a valuable skill they can use for the rest of their lives.

Handwriting is not taught as much, or in the same way, as it once was in American schools of the '20s and '30s. It has been further deemphasized within the past ten years when students began spending more time on computers. Perhaps one day schools will bypass cursive writing altogether and simply have students progress from manuscript writing straight to keyboarding. In the meantime, handwriting is a skill important enough to address. Whatever writing form your students prefer, help them to make it legible, striking a balance between the computer age and traditional handwriting.

Speaking

Speaking is oral composition of words, just as writing is written composition of words. It will help your student's writing if he or she is given plenty of opportunities to talk. Sometimes, just let your student tell a story or describe something. Encourage the development of ideas and use of new words. Do not, under any circumstances, make fun or joke about a student's wrong word use—sometimes permit it, and other times gently suggest a more correct word use. It is through experimenting and trying out that we all learned to talk and are likely still learning because, like reading and writing, speaking is a lifelong developmental process. So encourage the use of new or partially known words. Encourage wild or off-beat ideas as well as conventional ones. Take some time to just listen to your student. Some of the worst teachers are those who talk all the time.

Incidentally, don't be concerned about students' errors in speech sounds, especially in learners who are not native speakers of English. These students, often referred to as ESL (English as a Second Language) students, often have trouble pronouncing all of the sounds used in English because every language has its own set of speech sounds, some of which are not used in English. Spanish, for example, has no /j/ sound heard at the beginning of the Spanish word *general*; to native speakers of English it sounds like *heneral*. The name *Juan* sounds to English speakers as if it begins with a /wh/ sound. Certain Asian languages, such as Chinese, have no /l/ sound, so native speakers of that language usually pronounce the word *luck* as *ruck*.

Nonnative English speakers can improve their English pronunciation by practicing selected phonics patterns. (The Phonics Charts in Step 5 can provide some practice words for most speech sounds in English.) When working with these students, it is very important never to cause them any embarrassment. Speech sound production is based on mechanical mouth positions and breath, and you can often help correct speech errors by simply letting the student see you form the letters, then having the student look in a mirror as he or she makes the same sound. Once the student sees the correct placement of the tongue to form a certain sound, he can gradually substitute the new speech pattern for the old one by practicing words that have the troublesome sound.

Listening

As small children, we all learned to talk by listening. If the native language of our family and friends were Chinese, we would all speak Chinese. Beyond this basic fact, listening to material that is read helps students improve their speaking, reading, and writing. It is no surprise, therefore, that many educators recommend that you read to your students—and often. Take about ten minutes at every lesson to read to your students and just let them enjoy the sound of language modeled in flowing phrases.

Many good parents start off reading daily to their preschoolers—an excellent idea—but, unfortunately, they stop when the child starts elementary school. Even into the middle and upper grades you can read entire books to students, a little at a time, and students really enjoy it. No one is ever too old to listen. In fact, there are a number of storytelling festivals around the country whose audience is comprised mainly of adults. Also consider the many successful companies that sell books on tape. They sell these tapes not to the sight impaired or to those with no reading skills or to young children—but to working adults who listen to them in their cars while commuting or at home as they get ready for work. Most public libraries lend out audiocassettes of popular novels, short stories, and other titles covering a variety of interesting subjects.

Although books and stories usually come to mind first as choices for listening experiences, you can also read other kinds of material, including news or sports articles, advice columns, or directions to be followed—anything of interest to your student.

Listening is good for students for these reasons:

- It improves their vocabulary. Students hear language used well and hear words that might not appear in everyday speech.

- It improves their grammar. Students hear correct usage and variety in sentence construction.

- It broadens their horizon. Students are temporarily transported to the world of adventure or science fiction, to different countries, or to families and human experiences that are different from their own. They learn that language can be fun.

- They can listen to stories more difficult than those they can read for themselves and thus expand the choice of material. However, you can encourage students to set as their long-term goal of instruction the ability to read for themselves anything they can understand by listening.

If you do nothing else suggested in this book, that is, if you don't give any tests, teach any phonics or Instant Words, ask any comprehension questions, or assign any written stories or paragraphs, the least you can do is read to your student.

STEP 6 RESOURCES

Story Starters

Use the suggested story titles below for a topic, or choose from among these opening and closing phrases for an interesting first or last sentence, or answer in writing one of the questions listed. Also review items from the student Interest Inventory on pages 19–21 for other possible topics.

Titles

A Family Memory

My Best Friend

Curing the Blues

The Perfect Job

My Fifteen Minutes of Fame

The Baby Checks In

My Pet Peeve

A Shopper's Paradise

If I Ruled the World

A Home of My Own

Winning the Lottery

My Personal Hero

A Perfect Date

The Me That Nobody Knows

My Fantasy Vacation

The Midnight Visitor

A Stress-Filled Day

My Best Quality

The Spectacular Game

My Neighborhood

Story Openers

Someone who changed my life was . . .

I get mad when . . .

I'd give anything to meet . . .

People think that I . . .

I want to know more about . . .

With my children, I'll never . . .

The happiest I have ever been . . .

The worst driving habits are . . .

One thing that really bores me is . . .

My worst nightmare was . . .

The hardest thing I ever did was . . .

I promised to keep the secret, but . . .

I can hardly wait to . . .

My most prized possession is . . .

The day my car broke down . . .

I was afraid to admit that . . .

My child is special because . . .

I like to relax by . . .

The most important thing my parents taught me was . . .

I just bought a new . . .

The last good movie I saw was . . .

My New Year's resolution will be . . .

Nothing ever scared me more than . . .

Story Enders

That finally persuaded me to give up smoking.
That is a day I'd like to forget.
It was a day I'll always remember.
Now it has become a family joke.
This event has changed my life forever.
That's the last time I'll ever invite them over.
It cost a lot of money, but it was worth it.
Obviously I made the wrong choice (or the right choice).
Then the lights went out.
That's how he/she earned that nickname.
Now my friends say I should be a race car driver.
Everything he had said was a boldfaced lie.
To this day, I won't eat that food.
Now you can understand why I was so angry.
That was the end of a miserable week.
We'll never go back there again.
I was tired but happy.
That's when I realized I was an adult.
It was the worst vacation we ever had.
I finally decided to forgive and forget.

Good Questions

How is watching a game on television different from attending one in person?
What century would you like to live in?
What are the advantages and/or disadvantages of having a child?
What is the most interesting place you've ever visited? Why?
If you could change your house, what would it be like?
What could make you very happy or very sad?
What is an average day in your life like?
If you could change anything about your life, what would it be?
What would you like to be famous for and why?
Do you think the average person has the ability to make a lot of money?
How would your friends describe you?
What is your favorite fairy tale (or cartoon or TV show)?
What famous person from the past do you admire and why?
Who is your favorite entertainer? Why?
What will you do when you retire?
What would you do today if you could do anything you wanted?
Have you ever read a book that changed your life?
What accomplishment are your proudest of?
What new skill have you learned recently and what was difficult about it?

Handwriting Charts

Zaner-Bloser Manuscript Alphabet

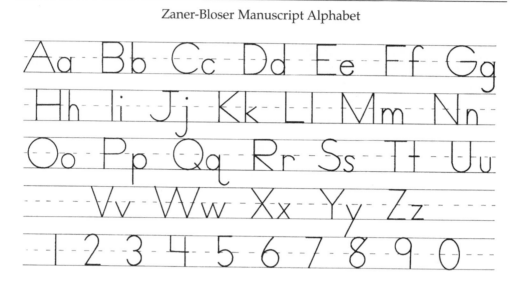

Zaner-Bloser Cursive Alphabet

Used with permission from Zaner-Bloser, Inc.

Conclusion and Sample Lessons

The ideal basic book about teaching reading should be long enough to cover the subject yet short enough to still be interesting. It is hoped that this one has met those criteria, but most college and public libraries as well as area resource centers for adult learning have plenty of books, journals, and other materials to aid your development as a teacher or tutor.

The preceding six steps present the basic techniques used by many experienced reading teachers. They should provide enough information to help you start teaching reading, but they also contain additional suggestions to improve your methods if you already have some teaching experience.

■ Additional Suggestions

The suggestions below are taken from a book entitled *The 10 Best Ideas for Reading Teachers*, in which forty-four nationally recognized reading experts offer some of their best ideas about teaching reading. Although practically every idea covered in the preceding chapters was mentioned by several of those reading specialists, you and your students might want to try out the additional ideas listed here.

Among the Best

- Use reading materials from other content areas, such as science or social studies.
- Include dramatic material (plays) for oral reading, speaking, and listening experiences.
- Write something every day. For example, keep a journal or diary.
- Write summaries of what you read. Write a letter to a friend.
- Teachers and tutors themselves should set a good example by reading often. Set aside regular, quiet times for reading.
- Use graphic organizers such as time lines for history, flow charts of a story or nonfiction selection, or clusters of characteristics associated with a particular vocabulary word.
- Encourage students to use a typewriter or computer for story writing. (If they do, teach your students to type using the 10-finger method.)

- Join a book club.

- Try reading the captions on television programs.

- Reread the same story several times, not just until oral errors disappear but to build reasonable speed and fluency as well.

- Occasionally repeat assessment tasks, such as the Oral and Silent Reading Tests and the Phonics Survey.

- If you spot reading problems, tackle them early on; waiting will only make them worse.

- Read for pleasure; read about real events; and read environmental print and trade names, such as Coca-Cola, Kleenex, and so on.

- Help expand students' vocabulary any way you can: by wide reading, speaking, and picking words from reading selections to discuss.

- Emphasize comprehension. Form questions before, during, and after reading. Ask questions that require the student to recall, summarize, and compare and contrast.

- Before reading a particular selection, draw on your student's prior knowledge and experience to develop background; talk about the setting, the characters, similarity in circumstance or in subject matter.

- All learners are individuals. They develop at different rates, have different interests, and have different abilities.

- Get a joke book. Read a joke every day. (For some very funny jokes on universal themes, try the two-book set *Comedy Comes Clean, A Hilarious Collection of Wholesome Jokes, Quotes, and One-Liners* and *Comedy Comes Clean 2*, compiled by Adam Christing and published by Three Rivers Press, New York.)

- Realize that learning to read is a complex, lifelong process. You are not going to develop a mature reader in one month or even one year, but you can certainly move your student ahead a notch in that length of time, and that, in the end, is all any teacher can do.

■ Sample Lessons

You have been exposed to plenty of ideas on how to teach reading, but exactly how do you start? What does a lesson consist of? Here are a few sample lessons for two students reading at different ability levels.

Student 1
Danita is a very beginning reader. She has almost no reading ability.

Student 2
James has some reading ability. He reads at about the third or fourth grade equivalency level.

Danita—Beginning Activities

1. Give Danita the Oral Reading Test (page 108). She scores Frustration Level at section 1-A.
2. Help Danita fill out an Interest Inventory (page 19). If it goes too slowly, take two or three sessions together to complete it.
3. She dictates a story (pages 91–92) for you to write on an experience chart.

   Limit chart story to a title and two short sentences.

   Limit words used—take mostly from first ten Instant Words (page 50) and first ten Picture Nouns (page 58).
4. Danita rereads the chart story several times for fluency.
5. She helps you make a simple Bingo game (page 43).
6. She makes two Bingo cards using good printing (page 100), and you make two cards. Each card has nine words (three columns, three rows) from chart story words.
7. The two of you play Bingo.
8. You read part of a book to Danita that is consistent with her interests.
9. You ask her some questions based on the book (see Comprehension Questions pages 30–31).
10. Give Danita positive feedback for her good work.

Danita's Next Lesson

1. Danita rereads yesterday's experience chart. You help her with words she has forgotten.
2. Add two new short sentences to the chart story. Danita suggests sentences; you write. Try to use a few more first ten words from Instant Words and Picture Nouns.
3. Danita rereads the story several times to improve fluency.
4. You take one of the words from story and show her it can be a phonogram. For example, -it can become *hit* and *sit*.
5. Have Danita write a *b* and an *m* before -*it*.
6. Play Bingo again with yesterday's cards.
7. Give Danita a five-word spelling test using chart story and phonogram words.
8. Correct the test paper and have Danita study the words missed.
9. Read more of the reading book to Danita.
10. Ask her questions about the story.
11. Continue with encouragement and positive feedback for her good work.

Danita's future lessons include

1. Continue building on components from previous lessons.

2. Soon introduce books for Danita to read with your help. (See Reading Materials, Step 2, pages 14–16.)

3. Danita should soon try writing a short story or experience with your help.

4. You or Danita can make a set of flash cards for words learned and new Instant Words.

5. After every few lessons you should reread sections of this book to make sure you build enough variety into student lessons.

James—Beginning Activities

1. Give Oral Reading Test (page 108). He scores Instructional Level at section 3-B.

2. Help James begin filling out an Interest Inventory (page 19). If it goes too slowly, take two or three lessons to complete it.

3. Give James the Instant Word Test (pages 56–57).

4. Play the Pairs game with James (page 44).

5. Read to James part of a book on a subject that interests him. (See Reading Materials, Step 2, pages 14–16.)

6. Get James to talk about what you've read by asking him some discussion questions (pages 30–31).

7. Make positive remarks to James for being so cooperative.

James's Next Lesson

1. Bring some books to your session based on Oral Test results (3rd grade difficulty) and based on his interest inventory. You and James select one and talk about it, building background for the content using James's prior knowledge and experience.

2. Help him read a small section of the book orally.

3. Have him reread the section silently.

4. Have him answer two questions orally and two questions by writing. (See Types of Questions, pages 30–31, and Vary the Ways to Respond, pages 34–35.)

5. Do all or part of the Phonics Survey (Step 5, page 73).

6. Use the Phonics Chart with example words on an error discovered in results of James's Phonics Survey.

7. Read to James from yesterday's book.

8. Give James plenty of positive feedback for the progress he's made so far.

James's Future Lessons Include

1. Continuation and extension of elements from Lessons 1 and 2. These are:

   Practice reading

   Improve vocabulary

   Learn phonics

   Teach comprehension

2. Have James write some stories, personal experiences, grocery lists, and so on.

3. Spelling lessons based on words he needed while writing and the Instant Word List. (See spelling suggestions in Step 4, page 46.)

4. Vocabulary building based on words in stories and on roots (Step 4, pages 62–63).

5. Use variety in James's reading instruction books and in the books from which you read to him (Step 3, Vary the Subject Matter, pages 28–29) or that he listens to on his own (Step 6, Listening, pages 96–97).

6. Give James plenty of encouragement and positive feedback.

■ The Last Word

No mention was made that Danita, who reads almost nothing, is a good deal older than James. But it doesn't matter, because one very important idea is to base the start of instruction on the student's current reading level, not on his or her age. Another important point, which cannot be overstressed, is to move your student ahead in steps small enough for him or her to be continually successful at each one, because the learner's success is your success too.

Rather than reading a summary of this book, you might be better served by rereading the one-paragraph description of how to teach reading (page 1) and the Overview of the book, beginning on the same page.

For students and teachers alike, there is no substitute for practice. Students, if they are to succeed, should commit to attending lessons and doing some reading practice at home. Teachers and tutors, after some initial preparation, should begin working with a student. Learning by doing is a great way to develop and improve teaching techniques. After coming face-to-face with a student's real-life reading problems and then rereading applicable portions of the book, you may find those sections a good deal more meaningful than at first glance.

Lastly, remember that the ability to teach reading is a wonderful skill. When you teach someone to read or to improve their reading skills, you have given that person a priceless gift that will keep on giving for a lifetime.

Appendix

Oral Reading Test

Directions:

Make photocopies of both the Examiner Copy and Record Sheet (pages 110–113) and the Student Copy of the test (pages 108–109). Ask the student to read aloud from a Student Copy starting with the test paragraph you choose for him. You will mark the Examiner Copy.

Scoring. Count one mistake for each word the student is unable to pronounce. If he immediately corrects himself, do not count the word as a mistake. If the student can't pronounce a word, or mispronounces it, just say "Go on." Do not tell the student the missed word or give him hints. If the student omits a word, ask him to read the line again more carefully.

Underline each word the student can't pronounce or needs help in pronouncing. When he finishes reading a paragraph, count the mistakes. Then, on the Examiner Copy, to the right of the test paragraph, check the box (in the *1st Testing* column) next to the appropriate reading level (*Independent, Instructional,* or *Frustration*). For example, if a student begins with Paragraph 1-B and reads it without a mistake, or with 1 or 2 mistakes (as shown in the *Errors* column), he can read at this level independently. Check the box next to *Indep.*

The student should then read Paragraph 2-A. If he gets a score of 0–2 mistakes, he can handle material at this level independently too. Check the box next to *Indep.*

He next reads Paragraph 2-B. If he makes 3-4 mistakes, you have found the student's Instructional Reading Level. Check the box next to *Instr.* This is the level at which reading instruction will be most effective for your student.

Notice that to the right of each paragraph on the Examiner Copy, the number of mistakes for the three reading levels is shown (the Errors column). However, the number of mistakes that determines a particular reading level (Independent,

Instructional, or Frustration) varies, depending on the grade level. For example, in Paragraphs 1-A through 2-B, 3 to 4 mistakes yield a student's Instructional Reading Level. But in Paragraphs 3-A and 3-B, 2 to 3 mistakes give the Instructional Reading Level, and only 2 mistakes do so in Paragraphs 4 through 7.

After finding the student's Instructional Reading Level, continue the test until you find his Frustration Reading Level. In Paragraphs 3-A and 3-B, 4 mistakes or more in a single paragraph would yield his Frustration Reading Level. But in Paragraphs 4 through 7, he would reach that level at just 3 mistakes or more. Stop testing when you get to the student's Frustration Level.

Record the test results (*Total Score*) in the space provided on the first page of the Examiner Copy. Note the highest grade level of material that should be used with the student for instruction.

Speed. The test paragraphs are not timed, but excessive rapidity or slowness in reading may be noted on the Examiner Copy to the right of the paragraph (next to *Speed*) as an important characteristic of the student's reading ability. Slow reading means that the student needs additional practice at that level to gain fluency.

Grade Equivalency Levels. There are two test paragraphs per grade equivalency level for grades 1 through 3. The first paragraph is marked 1-A. This means "easy first grade." The next is marked 1-B. This means "hard first grade."

There is only one paragraph for each grade level beyond third grade.

The last paragraph, labeled "7th Grade," is actually indicative of material at general adult and nonacademic or nontechnical secondary reading levels. A student who can read this level flawlessly can handle most junior- and senior-level high school readings satisfactorily. If the student reads the 7th Grade paragraph at the Independent Level, a standard silent reading test for a more accurate determination of advanced skills is recommended.

Note: DO NOT use this test for instruction. If you stick to this policy, you can use the same test at later dates to determine student progress. When retesting a student, underline mistakes using a different color pencil on the same Examiner Copy for that student. Spaces have been provided on the first page of the test for recording results of the second and third retesting. Keep the Examiner Copy/Record Sheet for quick reference and for retesting.

Oral Reading Test

No. 1-A

Look at the dog.
It is big.
It can run.
Run dog, run away.

No. 1-B

We saw the sun.
It made us warm.
Now it was time to go home.
It was a long way to walk.

No. 2-A

The door of the house opened and a man came out. He had a broom in his hand. He said to the boy sitting there, "Go away." The boy got up and left.

No. 2-B

The family ate their breakfast. Then they gave the pig his breakfast. It was fun to watch him eat. He seemed to like it. He is eating all of it.

No. 3-A

When the man had gone, the boys were surprised to see how many boxes he had left in their little back yard. Right away they began to pile them on top of each other. They made caves and houses. It took so long that lunch time came before they knew they were hungry.

No. 3-B

The man became angry because his dog had never talked before, and besides, he didn't like its voice. So he took his knife and cut a branch from a palm tree and hit his dog. Just then the palm tree said, "Put down that branch." The man was getting very upset about the way things were going, and he started to throw the branch away.

No. 4

Three more cowboys tried their best to rope and tie a calf as quickly as Red, but none of them came within ten seconds of his time. Then came the long, thin cowboy. He was the last one to enter the contest.

No. 5

High in the hills they came to a wide ledge where trees grew among the rocks. Grass grew in patches, and the ground was covered with bits of wood from trees blown over a long time ago and dried by the sun. Down in the valley it was already beginning to get dark.

No. 6

Businessmen from suburban areas may travel to work in helicopters, land on the roof of an office building, and thus avoid city traffic jams. Families can spend more time at summer homes and mountain cabins through the use of this marvelous craft. People on farms can reach city centers quickly for medical service, shopping, entertainment, or sale of products.

No. 7

The President of the United States was speaking. His audience comprised two thousand foreign-born men who had just been admitted to citizenship. They listened intently, their faces aglow with the light of a newborn patriotism, upturned to the calm, intellectual face of the first citizen of the country they now claimed as their own.

Oral Reading Test

To Determine Independent and Instructional Reading Levels
Examiner Copy and Record Sheet

Student's Name _____

Date _____

Class _____

	1st Testing	2nd Testing	3rd Testing
Date	_____	_____	_____
Total Score: Independent Reading Level	_____	_____	_____
	Grade	Grade	Grade
Instructional Reading Level	_____	_____	_____
	Grade	Grade	Grade

No. 1-A (Easy 1st Grade)	Errors	Level	1st Testing	2nd Testing	3rd Testing
Look at the dog.	0–2	Indep.	☐	☐	☐
It is big.	3–4	Instr.	☐	☐	☐
It can run.	5+	Frust.	☐	☐	☐
Run dog, run away.	Speed:	Fast	☐	☐	☐
		Avg.	☐	☐	☐
		Slow	☐	☐	☐
		V. Slow	☐	☐	☐

No. 1-B (Hard 1st Grade)	Errors	Level	1st Testing	2nd Testing	3rd Testing
We saw the sun.	0–2	Indep.	☐	☐	☐
It made us warm.	3–4	Instr.	☐	☐	☐
Now it was time to go home.	5+	Frust.	☐	☐	☐
It was a long way to walk.	Speed:	Fast	☐	☐	☐
		Avg.	☐	☐	☐
		Slow	☐	☐	☐
		V. Slow	☐	☐	☐

		1st Testing	2nd Testing	3rd Testing

No. 2-A (Easy 2nd Grade)

The door of the house opened and a man came out. He had a broom in his hand. He said to the boy sitting there, "Go away." The boy got up and left.

Errors	Level	1st Testing	2nd Testing	3rd Testing
0–2	Indep.	☐	☐	☐
3–4	Instr.	☐	☐	☐
5+	Frust.	☐	☐	☐
Speed:	Fast	☐	☐	☐
	Avg.	☐	☐	☐
	Slow	☐	☐	☐
	V. Slow	☐	☐	☐

No. 2-B (Hard 2nd Grade)

The family ate their breakfast. Then they gave the pig his breakfast. It was fun to watch him eat. He seemed to like it. He is eating all of it.

Errors	Level	1st Testing	2nd Testing	3rd Testing
0–2	Indep.	☐	☐	☐
3–4	Instr.	☐	☐	☐
5+	Frust.	☐	☐	☐
Speed:	Fast	☐	☐	☐
	Avg.	☐	☐	☐
	Slow	☐	☐	☐
	V. Slow	☐	☐	☐

No. 3-A (Easy 3rd Grade)

When the man had gone, the boys were surprised to see how many boxes he had left in their little back yard. Right away they began to pile them on top of each other. They made caves and houses. It took so long that lunch time came before they knew they were hungry.

Errors	Level	1st Testing	2nd Testing	3rd Testing
0–1	Indep.	☐	☐	☐
2–3	Instr.	☐	☐	☐
4+	Frust.	☐	☐	☐
Speed:	Fast	☐	☐	☐
	Avg.	☐	☐	☐
	Slow	☐	☐	☐
	V. Slow	☐	☐	☐

No. 3-B (Hard 3rd Grade)

The man became angry because his dog had never talked before, and besides, he didn't like its voice. So he took his knife and cut a branch from a palm tree and hit his dog. Just then the palm tree said, "Put down that branch." The man was getting very upset about the way things were going, and he started to throw the branch away.

Errors	Level	1st Testing	2nd Testing	3rd Testing
0–1	Indep.	☐	☐	☐
2–3	Instr.	☐	☐	☐
4+	Frust.	☐	☐	☐
Speed:	Fast	☐	☐	☐
	Avg.	☐	☐	☐
	Slow	☐	☐	☐
	V. Slow	☐	☐	☐

No. 4 (4th Grade)

Three more cowboys tried their best to rope and tie a calf as quickly as Red, but none of them came within ten seconds of his time. Then came the long, thin cowboy. He was the last one to enter the contest.

Errors	Level	1st Testing	2nd Testing	3rd Testing
0–1	Indep.	☐	☐	☐
2	Instr.	☐	☐	☐
3+	Frust.	☐	☐	☐
Speed:	Fast	☐	☐	☐
	Avg.	☐	☐	☐
	Slow	☐	☐	☐
	V. Slow	☐	☐	☐

No. 5 (5th Grade)

High in the hills they came to a wide ledge where trees grew among the rocks. Grass grew in patches, and the ground was covered with bits of wood from trees blown over a long time ago and dried by the sun. Down in the valley it was already beginning to get dark.

Errors	Level	1st Testing	2nd Testing	3rd Testing
0–1	Indep.	☐	☐	☐
2	Instr.	☐	☐	☐
3+	Frust.	☐	☐	☐
Speed:	Fast	☐	☐	☐
	Avg.	☐	☐	☐
	Slow	☐	☐	☐
	V. Slow	☐	☐	☐

No. 6 (6th Grade)

Businessmen from suburban areas may travel to work in helicopters, land on the roof of an office building, and thus avoid city traffic jams. Families can spend more time at summer homes and mountain cabins through the use of this marvelous craft. People on farms can reach city centers quickly for medical service, shopping, entertainment, or sale of products.

Errors	Level	1st Testing	2nd Testing	3rd Testing
0–1	Indep.	☐	☐	☐
2	Instr.	☐	☐	☐
3+	Frust.	☐	☐	☐
Speed:	Fast	☐	☐	☐
	Avg.	☐	☐	☐
	Slow	☐	☐	☐
	V. Slow	☐	☐	☐

No. 7 (7th Grade)

The President of the United States was speaking. His audience comprised two thousand foreign-born men who had just been admitted to citizenship. They listened intently, their faces aglow with the light of a newborn patriotism, upturned to the calm, intellectual face of the first citizen of the country they now claimed as their own.

Errors	Level	1st Testing	2nd Testing	3rd Testing
0–1	Indep.	☐	☐	☐
2	Instr.	☐	☐	☐
3+	Frust.	☐	☐	☐
Speed:	Fast	☐	☐	☐
	Avg.	☐	☐	☐
	Slow	☐	☐	☐
	V. Slow	☐	☐	☐

Silent Reading Comprehension Tests

How to Administer the Tests

Both tests are located on pages 116–124. If the test is to be administered to a group, make copies of the test at the students' appropriate level and give each student a copy. (A single student taking the test may do so right from this book and write his or her answers on a separate sheet of paper.) Read the following directions with your students and then tell them to begin:

> Read the stories and questions about the stories. You are to read each story carefully and then fill in the space next to the *best* answer to the question. You may look back at a story if it helps you answer the question. Don't rush, but don't waste time either.

Scoring and Interpretation

These two reading comprehension tests are designed to give you a general idea of a student's comprehension ability in a short period of time. They are shorter than most regular comprehension tests and therefore not quite as precise. However, they are a good supplement to a teacher's subjective opinion. In each test, the first five questions are literal comprehension questions; the second five are inferential questions.

You can tell how your student compares with typical third level readers on Test A and with typical seventh level readers on Test B. The student's age or education level doesn't matter.

The **Answer Key** on the next page tells you which comprehension skill is tested (vocabulary, main idea, inference, and so on) for each item, as well as the percentage of students at levels three or seven who answered the item correctly. Such information gives you some idea of the item difficulty and the kinds of skills in which your student may be strong or weak.

A **total score** (total number of items correct) also gives a more general idea of your students' reading comprehension skills. A total score of 8 correct on Test A would be average for nine-year-olds, who would likely be in mid-third grade. A total score of 7 on Test B would be average for thirteen-year-olds, who would likely be in mid-seventh grade. You can see how your older teen and adult students do in comparison with these guideposts.

Reading comprehension improves with continued practice and lessons, so teach it for a period of time using the ideas in Step 3 and from the list of Reading Materials in Step 2. Then retest your students using these reading comprehension tests to see if their skills have improved.

Answer Key

Test A—intended for third grade students. A score of 8 correct, which is average for this group, indicates average third grade reading ability.

Item	Answer	Question Type	Percent of Success for Nine-Year-Olds (National Norms)
1	b	Vocabulary	92%
2	d	Reference	63%
3	d	Facts	86%
4	d	Organization	83%
5	e	Main Idea	84%
6	c	Inference	75%
7	b	Inference	86%
8	c	Inference	60%
9	c	Critical Reading	75%
10	a	Critical Reading	75%

Test B—intended for seventh grade students. A score of 7 correct, which is average for this group, indicates average mid-seventh grade reading ability.

Item	Answer	Question Type	Percent of Success for Thirteen-Year-Olds (National Norms)
1	b	Vocabulary	76%
2	c	Locating Details	74%
3	a	Reference	68%
4	d	Facts	90%
5	c	Main Idea/Organization	88%
6	b	Inference	86%
7	e	Inference	72%
8	e	Inference	55%
9	b	Critical Reading	56%
10	b	Critical Reading	50%

Silent Reading Comprehension

Test A—3rd Grade Equivalency Level
Student Copy

Student's Name _____

Date _____

Read the stories and questions about the stories. You are to read each story carefully and then mark the box next to the *best* answer to the question. You may look back at a story if it helps you answer the question. Don't rush, but don't waste time either.

1. **Read the stories and do what they ask you to do.**

   ☐ a. If you have EVER visited the Moon, fill in the box here.
   ☐ b. If you have NEVER visited the Moon, fill in the box here.

2. **You want to call Mr. Jones on the telephone. You look in the telephone book for this number. You would find it between which names?**

   ☐ a. Jackson and Jacobs
   ☐ b. Jacobs and James
   ☐ c. James and Johnson
   ☐ d. Johnson and Judson
   ☐ e. Judson and Justus
   ☐ f. I don't know.

3. **Read the story and complete the sentence that follows it.**

   The wind pushed the boat farther and farther out to sea. It started to rain and the fog grew thick. The boy and his father were lost at sea.

   The weather was

   ☐ a. calm
   ☐ b. dry
   ☐ c. sunny
   ☐ d. wet
   ☐ e. I don't know.

4. **Read the story and answer the question that follows it.**

The wind pushed the boat farther and farther out to sea. It started to rain and the fog grew thick. The boy and his father were lost at sea.

What happened FIRST in the story?

☐ a. It became foggy.
☐ b. It started to rain.
☐ c. The boat turned over.
☐ d. The boat went out to sea.
☐ e. I don't know.

5. **Read the passage and answer the question that follows it.**

A sports car differs from an ordinary passenger car in that its size and number of accessories are limited. The sports car also differs from the ordinary passenger car in performance. It can attain higher speeds because it is built smaller and lower. For these reasons, it can also turn corners faster and more smoothly than a passenger car. Also, a sports car generally gets better gas mileage than an ordinary passenger car.

What does the writer tell you about sports cars?

☐ a. prices
☐ b. colors and styles
☐ c. places to buy them
☐ d. number of people they hold
☐ e. how sports cars differ from passenger cars
☐ f. I don't know.

6. **This question is like a game to see if you tell what the nonsense word in the paragraph stands for. The nonsense word is just a silly word for something that you know very well. Read the paragraph and see if you can tell what the underlined nonsense word stands for.**

Most people have two cags. You use your cags to hold things when you eat or brush your teeth. Some people write with their right cag, and some people write with their left cag.

Cags are probably

☐ a. eyes
☐ b. feet
☐ c. hands
☐ d. pencils
☐ e. I don't know.

7. **Read the story and answer the question that follows it.**

   The wind pushed the boat farther and farther out to sea. It started to rain and the fog grew thick. The boy and his father were lost at sea.

   At least how many people were in the boat?

   ☐ a. one
   ☐ b. two
   ☐ c. three
   ☐ d. four
   ☐ e. five
   ☐ f. I don't know.

8. **Read the story and answer the question that follows it.**

   Christmas was only a few days away. The wind was strong and cold. The sidewalks were covered with snow. The downtown streets were crowded with people. Their faces were hidden by many packages as they went in one store after another. They all tried to move faster as they looked at the clock.

   When did the story probably happen?

   ☐ a. November 28
   ☐ b. December 1
   ☐ c. December 21
   ☐ d. December 25
   ☐ e. December 28
   ☐ f. I don't know.

9. **Read this story about a fish and answer the question that follows it.**

   Once there was a fish named Big Eyes, who was tired of swimming. He wanted to get out of the water and walk like other animals do. So one day without telling anyone, he just jumped out of the water, put on his shoes, and took a long walk around the park.

   What do you think the person who wrote this story was trying to do?

   ☐ a. tell you what fish are like
   ☐ b. tell you that fish wear shoes
   ☐ c. tell you a funny story about a fish
   ☐ d. tell you that fish don't like to swim
   ☐ e. I don't know.

10. If you listen carefully to what a person says, you can usually tell a lot about him or her. Sometimes you can tell how the person feels.

Read the passage and complete the sentence that follows it.

"I'll be glad when this TV show is over. I like stories about spies, not this one about cowboys and Indians. I get to pick the next show."

The person who said this

☐ a. likes spy stories
☐ b. doesn't like TV at all
☐ c. doesn't care what TV show is on
☐ d. likes stories about cowboys and Indians
☐ e. I don't know.

Total Score _____

Silent Reading Comprehension

Student's Name _____

Date _____

Below are a number of stories and questions about the stories. You are to read each story carefully and then mark the box next to the *best* answer to the question. You may look back at a story if it helps you answer the question. Don't rush, but don't waste time either.

1. **Read the sentence and mark the box beside the group of words that tells what the sentence means.**

    "I *certainly* won't miss that movie."

    ☐ a. I like that movie.
    ☐ b. I'm going to that movie.
    ☐ c. I'm not going to that movie.
    ☐ d. I hope I'll see that movie, but I don't know if I can.
    ☐ e. I didn't see that movie, although it was here all fall.
    ☐ f. I don't know.

2. **Read the directions from a can of insecticide spray and answer the question which follows them.**

    ABC Bug Spray

    Kills: spiders, roaches, ants, and most other crawling insects.
    Directions: Spray surfaces over which insects may crawl: doorways, window ledges, cracks, etc. Hold can approximately 10 inches from surface. Do not use near uncovered food or small children. Toxic.

    Which of the following will probably NOT be killed by the spray?

    ☐ a. ants
    ☐ b. caterpillars
    ☐ c. flies
    ☐ d. roaches
    ☐ e. spiders
    ☐ f. I don't know.

3. **What is the BEST way to find out if there is something about Eskimos in a book?**

   ☐ a. Look in the index.
   ☐ b. Look in the glossary.
   ☐ c. Look at the title page.
   ☐ d. Look through all the pages.
   ☐ e. Skim through the introduction.
   ☐ f. I don't know.

4. **Read the passage and answer the question that follows it.**

   It should come as no surprise to learn that 9 out of 10 Americans are in debt. In fact, 5 out of 10 are heavily in debt. How heavily is borne out by government statistics, which show that income has increased 50%—while debts have increased 110%!

   It is important to put statistics into their proper perspective: paying off the car, the home, the groceries, the doctors, and even the children's education is now a way of life for over a hundred million Americans. Very few of us could get by if we had to pay cash when we buy. Keeping up with the Joneses is made easier for us by easy payment plans, easy-to-acquire charge cards, and easy-to-borrow bank loans.

   According to the article, how many Americans are in debt?

   ☐ a. 50%
   ☐ b. 2 out of 3
   ☐ c. 4 out of 5
   ☐ d. 9 out of 10
   ☐ e. I don't know.

5. **Read the two stories and answer the question that follows them.**

STORY 1

   A handsome prince was riding his horse in the woods. He saw a dragon chasing a beautiful princess. The prince killed the dragon. The prince and the princess were then married.

STORY 2

   Mary was taking a boat ride on a lake. The boat tipped over. Mary was about to drown when a young man jumped in the lake and saved her.

If Story 2 ended like Story 1, what would happen next in Story 2?

☐ a. A prince would kill a dragon.
☐ b. The young man would become a prince.
☐ c. Mary and the young man would get married.
☐ d. The king would give the young man some money.
☐ e. I don't know.

6. **Read the story and answer the questions that follows it.**

   Sammy got to school ten minutes after the school bell had rung. He was breathing hard and had a black eye. His face was dirty and scratched. One leg of his pants was torn.
   Tommy was late to school, too; however, he was only five minutes late. Like Sammy, he was breathing hard, but he was happy and smiling.
   Sammy and Tommy had been fighting.

Who probably won?

☐ a. Sammy
☐ b. Tommy
☐ c. cannot tell from the story
☐ d. I don't know.

7. **Read the passage and answer the question that follows it.**

One spring, Farmer Brown had an unusually good field of wheat. Whenever he saw any birds in this field, he got his gun and shot as many of them as he could. In the middle of the summer, he found that the insects had multiplied very fast. What Farmer Brown did not understand was this: A bird is not simply an animal that eats food the farmer may want for himself. Instead, it is one of many links in the complex surroundings, or environment, in which we live.

How much grain a farmer can raise on an acre of ground depends on many factors. All of these factors can be divided into two big groups. Such things as the richness of the soil, the amount of rainfall, the amount of sunlight, and the temperature belong together in one of the groups. This group may be called <u>nonliving factors</u>. The second group may be called <u>living factors</u>. The living factors in any plant's environment are animals and other plants. Wheat, for example, may be damaged by wheat rust, a tiny plant that feeds on wheat; or it may be eaten by plant-eating animals such as birds or grasshoppers.

It is easy to see that the relations of plants and animals to their environment are very complex, and that any change in the environment is likely to bring about a whole series of changes.

What important idea about nature does the writer want us to understand?

☐ a. Farmer Brown was worried about the heavy rainfall.
☐ b. Nobody needs to have such destructive birds around.
☐ c. Farmer Brown didn't want the temperature to change.
☐ d. All insects need not only wheat rust but also grasshoppers.
☐ e. All living things are dependent on other living things.
☐ f. I don't know.

8. **Read the passage and complete the sentence that follows it.**

Art says that the polar ice cap is melting at the rate of 3% per year. Bert says that this isn't true because the polar ice cap is really melting at the rate of 7% per year.

We know for CERTAIN that

☐ a. Art is wrong.
☐ b. Bert is wrong.
☐ c. They are both wrong.
☐ d. They both might be right.
☐ e. They can't both be right.
☐ f. I don't know.

9. **Read the passage and answer the question that follows it.**

Johnny told Billy that he could make it rain any time he wanted to by stepping on a spider. Billy said Johnny couldn't. Johnny stepped on a spider. That night it rained. The next day Johnny told Billy, "That proves I can make it rain any time I want to."

Was Johnny right?

☐ a. yes
☐ b. no
☐ c. can't tell from the passage
☐ d. I don't know.

10. **Read the poem and answer the question that follows it.**

My body a rounded stone
With a pattern of smooth seams,
My head a short snake,
Retractive, protective.
My legs come out of their sleeves
Or shrink within,
And so does my chin.
My eyelids are quick clamps.

My back is my roof.
I am always at home.
I travel where my house walks.
It is a smooth stone.
It floats within the lake,
Or rests in the dust.
My flesh lives tenderly
Inside its home.

Which word BEST describes the speaker in the poem?

☐ a. confused
☐ b. contented
☐ c. excited
☐ d. restless
☐ e. unhappy
☐ f. I don't know.

Total Score _____

Important Words

Traffic Words and Signs

The words on these common signs are important for students to learn as sight words.

BRIDGE OUT	SLOW
RAILROAD CROSSING	SHARP CURVE
DEAD END	WALK
RIGHT TURN ONLY	EXIT ONLY
NO PARKING	PAY TOLL AHEAD
GASOLINE	NO PASSING
FOOD	ENTRANCE
LEFT LANE MUST TURN LEFT	JUNCTION
NO TURNS	TRUCK ROUTE
MERGING TRAFFIC	PAVEMENT ENDS
ROAD CLOSED	CAUTION
NO U TURN	NO LEFT TURN
NORTH	ROAD ENDS
SOUTH	DO NOT ENTER
EAST	TRAFFIC CIRCLE
WEST	HOSPITAL ZONE
CHILDREN CROSSING	DEER CROSSING
WEIGH STATION	THREE WAY STOP
CONSTRUCTION AHEAD	SCHOOL ZONE
FOUR-WAY STOP	FALLING ROCKS
DIVIDED HIGHWAY	SLIPPERY WHEN WET
REST ROOMS	NO STOPPING
TOWAWAY ZONE	LAST CHANCE FOR GAS
LOADING ZONE	PRIVATE ROAD
BUS ONLY	KEEP RIGHT
FREEWAY	LANE ENDS

Everyday Words

Danger

Acid
Alarm
Antidote
Blasting
Break Glass
Caution
Do Not Drink
Do Not Stand Up
Do Not Use
Down
Emergency Exit
Explosives
Fire Escape
Fire Extinguisher
First Aid
Flammable
Gas
Harmful if Swallowed
High Voltage
Hot
Keep Out
Keep Refrigerated
Live Power Supply
No Admittance
No Trespassing
Oxygen
Pedestrians
Radioactive
Railroad
Smoking Prohibited
Stairway
Stop—Blow Horn
Swim at Your Own Risk
Warning

Daily Living

Adults Only
Alcohol
Ambulance
Apartment
Automated Teller Machine
  (ATM)
Bank
Bus Stop
Cab
Cafeteria
Cash Station
Church
Cleaners
Closed
Cold
Credit Card
Customer Service
Dentist
Deposit 25¢
Dimes Only
Doctor
Elevator
Enter
First Aid
For Rent
For Sale
Fragile
Free
Gentlemen
Groceries
Handle with Care
Help Wanted
Hospital
Hot
Hotel
In/Out
Information

Ladies
Laundry
Library
Main Door
Men
Money
No Checks Cashed
No Dogs Allowed
No Smoking
Nurse
Office
Open
Operator
Out of Order
Phone
Physician
Police
Post Office
Public Parking
Pull
Push
Quarters Only
Quiet
School
Self-Service
Store
Subway
This Way Out
Toll
Train
Up
Down
Wanted
Women

Menu Words

Cheeseburger
Chili
Soup
Burritos
Ham and Cheese
Hamburger
Taco
Hot Dog
Meatball
Salad
Salad Dressing
Steak
Tuna Fish
Vegetable
Sandwich
Fruit
French Fries
Mashed Potatoes
Peas
Carrots
Broccoli
Pizza
Chicken
Fish
Roast Beef
Pork Chops
Turkey
Coffee
Tea
Iced Tea
Soft Drink
Milk
Cake
Pie
Ice Cream

Grocery/Drug

Aspirin
Baby Food
Bread
Butter
Margarine
Canned Food
Crackers
Cereal
Shortening
Eggs
Chocolate
Flour
Yogurt
Fruit
Juice
Meat
Pasta
Pepper
Corn
Pharmacy
Lettuce
Potatoes
Tomatoes
Rice
Salt
Plastic Wrap
Soap
Detergent
Sugar
Toothpaste
Paper Towels
Vegetables

Income Taxes

If Filing Joint Return
First Names
Middle Initial
Spouse's
Check One
Married Filing Joint
    Return
Married Filing Separately
Enter Total Wages
Tips
Interest
Dividends
Total Income Tax from Tax
    Table
Total Federal Income Tax
    Withheld
Larger Than
Balance Due
Refund
Dependent's Support
Amount Furnished
If Filing 100% Write "All"
Sign Here
Both Must Sign
Interest
Larger Than
Married
Withholding Allowances
Attached Certificate
Deductions Allowed
Exemptions
Itemized Deductions

Words and Phrases for Completing Forms

date
month
year
name
Mr.
Mrs.
Miss
Ms.
first name
last name
maiden name
middle name
middle initial
mother's maiden name
address
street
permanent address
mailing address
residence
city
state
zip code
telephone number
business telephone

home telephone
citizen
citizenship status
birthdate
date of birth
place of birth
age
height
weight
Social Security Number
marital status
married
separated
divorced
widowed
single
occupation
employer
firm
place of employment
length of service
references
in case of emergency
relationship

education
years of schooling
last school attended
degrees held
diplomas held
salary
hourly
weekly
part-time
full-time
temporary work
sex
male
female
health plan coverage
medical history
physical impairment
driver's license number
signature
insurance
dependents
work experience
describe work duties
reason for leaving

INDEX

BOOKS BY EDWARD FRY

Reading and Writing Handbooks
(Contemporary Books, Chicago, IL)

1000 Instant Words	teacher reference (1–3)
Phonics Patterns	teacher reference (1–3)
Introductory Word Book	1–4
Writer's Manual	4–8

Student Activity Skillbooks
(Contemporary Books, Chicago, IL)

Phonics and Whole Word Activity Book 1	1–2
Phonics and Whole Word Activity Book 2	2–3
Introductory Word Book Activity Book	3–4
Writer's Manual Activity Book 1	4–6
Writer's Manual Activity Book 2	6–8

Spelling Book, Words Most Needed Plus Phonics
(Teacher Created Materials, Westminster, CA)   1–6

Computer Keyboarding for Beginners
(Teacher Created Materials, Westminster, CA)   beginning

Picture Nouns (Teacher Created Materials, Westminster, CA)
Word and Picture Flash Cards   beginning and ESL

Fry Readability Scale (Jamestown Publishers, Chicago, IL)

Jamestown's Reading Improvement
(Jamestown Publishers, Chicago, IL)

Reading Drills Introductory Level	4–6
Reading Drills Intermediate Level	6–8
Reading Drills Advanced Level	7–10
Vocabulary Drills Intermediate Level	6–8
Vocabulary Drills Advanced Level	9–12
Skimming and Scanning Intermediate Level	4–6
Skimming and Scanning Advanced Level	7–10